Wide Awake Worship

Hymns and Prayers Renewed
for the 21st Century

Wide Awake Worship

Hymns and Prayers Renewed
for the 21st Century

John Henson

BOOKS

Winchester, UK
Washington, USA

First published by O-Books, 2010
O-Books is an imprint of John Hunt Publishing Ltd., Laurel House, Station Approach,
Alresford, Hants, SO24 9JH, UK
office1@o-books.net
www.o-books.com

For distributor details and how to order please visit the 'Ordering' section on our website.

Text copyright John Henson 2010

ISBN: 978 1 84694 392 8

A CIP catalogue record for this book is available from the British Library.

Design: Stuart Davies

Printed in the UK by CPI Antony Rowe
Printed in the USA by Offset Paperback Mfrs, Inc

We operate a distinctive and ethical publishing philosophy in all
areas of its business, from its global network of authors to
production and worldwide distribution.

CONTENTS

Section 2. Buttons Polished.

Foreword

I grew up in a congregation that used 'Congregational Praise' as a hymn book. It was first published in 1951 and the first lines of the preface said:

'The *Congregational Hymnary* was published in 1916. In the Preface it is stated that 'each generation requires – or, at least, demands – its own hymn-book.''

We used to laugh at that when we were still using Congregational Praise in 1989, when I started training for the ministry. That didn't mean that things had stood still. The language and style of worship changed considerably in the last decades of the twentieth century, and many congregations used supplements to their traditional hymn books, either printed or projected. It is simple: God continues to be involved in this changing world, and our response of worship, and the words of hymns, need to develop to keep up.

At the same time, hymns from the past help us to know where we have come from, and make us aware of the community of the Spirit of which we are part. I had a colleague who said, 'We don't sing any worship song that's more than five years old in our church.' Whilst that ensures a contemporary feel to worship, a hymn is not necessarily good just because it is new. Words and tunes and rhythms from our past help us to move into worship.

Amongst some churches the hymn book tended to be seen as the prayer book for the congregation, they were arranged thematically and hymns were seen as a source of private devotion as well as corporate worship. Now hymn books are more likely to be arranged alphabetically by their first line, but they still express theology. I've always been impressed by the way that John Bell of the Iona community combines refreshing theology with new tunes or with old folk tunes that strike a deep chord. His conviction that we start 'to believe what we sing' shows the importance of reviewing the hymns and songs we use in worship and test whether they express what we believe.

The hymns that John Henson has collected here resonate with these thoughts. John sometimes takes an established hymn and uses the themes and tune to give familiarity, but uses fresh words to update the theology. He sometimes takes a hymn which has given a false impression for years, and writes new verses to reflect recent scholarship. Always they are about praising God in whom we have faith, in words that reflect the faith we have.

These hymns may not all suit you. You might not be able to imagine singing them in your church. Hopefully you will find them thought and faith provoking, and use them as a way into prayer. Maybe they will even encourage you to try adapting or writing a hymn yourself. Then they will have done their job of prompting worship of God.

Simon Walkling. Minister St. David's Uniting Church, Pontypridd.

Introduction

'Sing heartily, by all means, but think carefully about what you're singing.' Letters to Corinth. Good As New pg 346

Gems Reset and Buttons Polished arose out of the concern of many Christians who have told me they find it difficult to join in the traditional prayers and hymns of the churches with honesty since the words no longer accurately express their genuine beliefs and commitment. Yet at the same time is felt a sense of loss that is more than just nostalgia for the tools of devotion of former years. Is there something that can be rescued from these hymns and prayers? The tunes, surely. But are the words all dross? Can we strip away the militarism, triumphalism, imperialism, flat-earthism, exclusivism, sexism and sentimentalism with which many of the great hymns and prayers are marred? Here we try. Whether we succeed or not, whether there is a market for such a product, time alone will tell. Maybe it will be up to others to do better than we have done. Indeed there are many others already working in this field.

For some our efforts may simply create a new awareness. The new settings and polishing may get them to realise that much of what they say and sing in their churches is twaddle and that by continuing they are slowly sawing through the cord that connects faith with reality. The church that encourages its people to sing over and over again words that do not have the ring of truth is doing something very dangerous. It is not only endangering its own future, but damaging the psyche of lovely people, and that is very bad indeed.

These reset gems and polished buttons are dedicated to my father, Revd. W. Clifford Henson who had a special love for the great hymns of the Church and introduced hymns of quality, both old and new, in the churches of Wales and the South West of England where he ministered. He believed we were expected by God to use our minds in worship, and among his pet hates were songs with trite poetry, shallow theology and weak tunes. He would certainly have agreed with the purpose of this book. Whether he would have been satisfied with its contents is less certain. We shall have to wait until we see him again to find out.

John Henson, compiler.

Gems Reset

The Beauty

('The Grace')

The beauty of Jesus our Leader, the Love of God our Parent, and the Joy of the Spirit our Uniter be with us for ever. Amen (Or 'Be it so' or 'Yes')

Ready for God

('*Prayer of Humble Access*')

(*Alternative responses as above*)

Loving God, you know our thoughts, our feelings and our secrets. You accept us as we are. Fuse your Spirit with our minds and passions to make our love real and our thanks sincere. We meet you through Jesus, our Leader.
Or (Closer to trad)
All loving God, to whom all hearts are open, all desires known, and from whom no secrets are hidden:
Cleanse the thoughts of our hearts by the inspiration of your Spirit, that we may truly love you and sincerely praise you for what you are.

The Pattern Prayer

('The Lord's Prayer')

Loving God, here and everywhere, help us proclaim your values and bring in your New World. Supply us with our day to day needs. Forgive us for wounding you, while we forgive those who wound us. Give us courage to meet life's trials and deal with evil's power. We celebrate your New World, full of life and beauty, lasting forever.

Passing on the Goodness

(The Levitical Blessing)

God cheer you and look after you; God convince you that life is good; God assure you that love is the lasting reality; God satisfy your deepest needs; God give you peace, now and forever.

Friends Not Servants

(Prayer of Ignatius Loyola)

Teach us, Jesus, to help you all we can; to give without
resentment more than we intended; to love and accept love and
cope with its pain; to enjoy work, rest and play; to be friends
you can rely on; for your sake and ours. Amen (Or 'Be it so' or
'Yes')

Duet for Heaven and Earth

('The Gloria')

Enjoy God's beauty above and around,
And share God's peace with every living thing.
Our God and eternal Friend,
Mother and Father of all,
We value you, we thank you
We praise you for your love.

Jesus, faithful likeness of God,
True God, God given as a present to us,
You remove the world's misery and mess:
Help us and comfort us;
You share our full humanity:
We know you listen.

For only you are genuine;
Only you are pure love,
Only you are worth everything else and more;
Jesus, God's character, with the Spirit, God's presence,
The beauty of God for all to enjoy.

Mary's Song for Lisa (Elizabeth)

('The Magnificat' As in 'Good As New')

I sense the greatness of God
Who makes my joy complete;
God smiled at me and asked my help,
And everyone will dance with glee
At the wonderful thing happening to me.
What a God!

In every age God helps the good,
Upsetting the plans of the arrogant:
See how the powerful fall off their perches!
Honor for the modest, a banquet for the hungry;
The rich get nothing and slink away!
God keeps promises to friends and companions -
Abraham, Sarah, and their like today.

Simeon's Goodbye

(The 'Nunc Dimittis')

Now God your helper is ready to move on,
Because I have seen your plan for the world.
Soon the secret will be out -
New hope for every land,
The greatest event in your people's history.
OR
(As in 'Good As New')
Your helper, God, moves on content,
Your plans my eyes have seen;
A new day dawns for every land,
Beyond your people's dream.

Kerry's Song

('The Benedictus' – 'Song of Zechariah'
As in 'Good as New')

What a wonderful God,
The God of Jacob, Leah, and Rachel!
This God has come to help us and set us free.

The world will be healed by the power of love,
By a descendant of David and Bathsheba.
Those who spoke God's promises were right:
The days of hate and having enemies are passing.

God was generous to our ancestors,
A loyal and reliable friend.
God promised Abraham and Sarah
An end to hostility and fear,
Freedom to worship and serve.

You, little baby, will speak for God;
You will go in front of God's Chosen Leader
And roll out the carpet.
You'll tell people their problems are over,
Free from guilt at last.

God is kind and gentle;
God will turn darkness into daylight,
So we can make our way in peace.

Giving Credit where Credit's Due

('Te Deum Laudamus')

We praise you, God:
You are greater than everything.

The whole world marvels
At the one who loves forever.

All those close to you sing your praise:
Their songs echo through time and space.

Artists and musicians
Speak with one voice -

'Great, wise and beautiful God,
Lover of millions,

Everywhere your brilliance
Startles and surprises us.'

Those who announce your good news praise you:
Those who speak your words praise you.

Those who have died for you praise you:
Your friends the world over praise you.

All who know about your love
Through the one who is your Likeness,
With the help of your Spirit.

Jesus, you are the greatest of all;
You are the true likeness of the Loving God.
To save us from our folly,
You became one of us.

You did away with death and its horrors
And invited everybody to God's New World.

You are one with the being of God.
God's love shines through you.

We believe you will put right
Everything wrong with us.

So your friends look to you for help.
You have made us yours by dying for us.

Help us to be like you
And reflect your beauty.

God, heal your people and improve their lives;
Teach them to love and inspire them with confidence.

You seem greater to us every moment;
There is always more to learn about you.

Help us today to avoid being selfish;
We are glad you keep on forgiving.

Your kindness makes us want to please you.
Each says, 'I trust you God.
You will not let me down.'

Spreading the Word

(Introduction to readings from Hebrew writings, Early

Christian Writings and Post-Biblical writings)

Bidding before readings.

Listen to this reading from Jeremiah the Prophet
Listen to this reading of Good News from Mark
Listen to this reading from the words of Theresa of Lisieux
Response (optional) We are ready to listen.

Bidding after readings

Give thanks for every way God speaks!
Response (optional) We thank you God!
Or:

Bidding

Praise God who speaks to us!

Response

Amen.

Note. It has become fashionable in some quarters to precede the reading of the Bible with the words 'Hear the Word of God as found...etc' and to conclude with 'This is the Word of the Lord', to which the congregation are expected to reply 'Thanks be to God.' This form of words, besides sounding authoritarian , equates (intentionally or otherwise) the expression 'Word of God' with the Bible, thus excluding the recognition of the Word of God in later and contemporary Christian writings and the writings of other faiths, as well as through the physical universe, the arts, preaching, prayer, fellowship, etc. For the Christian, Jesus is paramount as 'The Word made Flesh'.

The forms suggested here provide a liturgical bidding and response to the reading of the scriptures and other writings in the context of Christian worship, **though readings can be more effective when allowed to speak for themselves, unadorned by liturgical frills.**

Joining In

(Simple responses for prayers for other people)

For the World.

Leader: God of all goodness
All: Use our prayer

For those close to us and for ourselves

Leader: Caring God
All: We bring our care

For all in need

Leader: Loving God
All: Hold them in your arms

Note. These examples are only suggestions of forms appropriate for the twenty-first century. Leaders of worship should experiment to discover the forms of words they feel most at ease with. They should always be **brief** for easy mind retention. 'Lord in your mercy - hear our prayer' is unacceptable since it retains the grovelling approach from days in which God was approached more in fear than love. God is not a deaf, medieval, tyrannical aristocrat!

Enjoying the Positive

(Book of Common Prayer - General Thanksgiving)

Loving God, our constant helper, we thank you for your goodness and kindness to us and to all. Thank you for our being here, for our life up to this moment, and for all we have received from you. We thank you most of all for your demonstration of love in Jesus. Through him you share your freedom with the whole world.

Thank you for our senses, for means of expression, and for the hopes and desires that link us to you. Help us to show our thanks, not just in words, but in the way we live. Help us to be your people, daring and different, keen to work alongside you. We worship you as we see you in Jesus and experience you through your Spirit. Your eternal love merits eternal thanks. We thank you now.

Amen (Or 'Be it so')

Shifting the Negative

(Book of Common Prayer - General Confession)

God, all-loving and all-kind, we have not always kept in touch with you; we have sometimes messed up our lives and spoiled the lives of others people; often our best projects have been flawed, and our highest ambitions come to nothing; we have acted from mixed motives and our generosity has been tinged with self-interest. We are amazed that you still love us and accept us.

Help us respond to your patience and understanding. Save us from despair or half-heartedness.

Deal with our nastiness, our pride and our intolerance, and replace them with your goodness and compassion. Let us feel the pain we cause others, and bring it to an end. Give us the sense to learn from our mistakes.

As you value us, teach us to value ourselves as your friends and helpers. You forbid us to wallow in feelings of guilt or unworthiness.

In partnership with you, may we experience new lives, new hopes, new responsibilities and new joys, seeing your New World come, inside us and around us.

Amen (Or 'Yes')

I Trust

(Creed - John Henson)

(*John Henson is a Baptist who doesn't hold with reciting or otherwise enforcing creeds, but who recommends every Christian to write down a summary of what they believe, and update it from time to time as The Spirit takes them forward.*)

I put my trust in God;
I trust that God is Love.
God is involved in everything.
God shoulders responsibility for everything;
God is male and female,
Personal and passionate;
God seeks friends.
God is active, creative, explorative;
God is strong and tender
With a great sense of humour.
God prefers to work in partnership
And takes risks.
God hates cruelty and unkindness
And sides with the wounded and oppressed.

I put my trust in Jesus -
God made known in a human person.
Jesus lived in Palestine
At the time of the Roman occupation.
He taught and healed
And proclaimed a New World;
He befriended outcasts.
This angered the religious and powerful

Who tortured and killed him.
To the end he showed God's love,
Dying with forgiveness on his lips.
His friends realised he had overcome death
And would be with them always.

I put my trust in God's Spirit;
Through her, the God of Jesus
May be known at all times and in all places.
She is sensed in music and art,
In all that is noble and beautiful,
Affectionate and understanding;
In the variety and movement of the natural order,
In human longing and aspiration.
She offers many pathways to God.

I trust that none is excluded from God's love;
For all there is hope everlasting.
Those who respond to God's love now
Anticipate the joyful meeting of God's loved and loving,
Past, present and future.

Advent Prayer

Loving God, help us to get rid of what's bad in us, and develop what's good in us; we want to make the best use of our time here on earth, where Jesus made his home, and with him share the life of those despised and rejected.

So that we may know the joy of your closeness, and experience the full life you have invited us to. Amen (Or 'So be it')

Christmas Day Prayer

All loving God, you have come to us in Jesus, your True
Likeness. You have been born as one of us, to be cared for and
brought up to adulthood by human parents.
We receive your invitation to join your family, together with
Mary and Joseph, and all the new members you are seeking and
embracing, year after year, day by day.
By following Jesus and through the workings of your Spirit,
help us to share your nature and to be truly yours.
Amen (Or 'Be it so')

Christmas Blessing

May the lovely man who once walked the dusty roads of the
Middle East be your constant companion; may he be the Prince
of Peace to your hearts, the word of calm to your troubled
minds, healing to your wounds, the end of all your loneliness;
let him turn outcast and victim into honoured guest; let him
demonstrate for you that love which is the very nature of God.
Then the goodness of God the Lover, the company of God the
Friend and the cheer of God the Merrrymaker will be with you
this Christmastime.
Amen (Or 'Yes')

The Visit of the Magicians

God, by the leading of a star you showed that you belong to all cultures and faiths. Help it to come about that we may follow our star in company with you, and so one day worship you in the company of those ancient magicians from Persia, and with all the many other varieties and types of people you delight in. Yes!

Prayers for Valentine's Day February 14th

(In Wales, 'Dwynwen' 25 January)

(1 John 4: 7-21 'Good As New' pg 430)
'Dear friends, let's love one another, because love is a present from God'

God who is love, and loves and inspires others to love, we pray today for all who love. For those who love passionately and deeply and with long term commitment, and for those who love hesitatingly, unsure and anxious, and for those who love recklessly without really understanding what they are doing or what has got hold of them.

All love comes from you. Even that love which we spoil with our selfishness and lust started with you. So we ask that you will strengthen those who love in your love, that they may be aware of your approval and encouragement.

We ask that you will help us to cleanse from our love those things which destroy love - jealousy and possessiveness, the desire to have our own way, the urge to exploit another for our own ends.

'Everyone who loves shares a family likeness with God and has a relationship with God.'

We pray for those who have recently made vows of marriage or have agreed to live together in a relationship, that they may walk life together with confidence and sensitivity to each others' needs. We pray for those who are planning marriage as they look forward with anticipation, that their great day may be joyful, and that friends and family may be drawn together in the love which the couple have found.

We pray for those who are encountering difficulties in their relationships - misunderstandings, boredom, tension and strain, that love may be rekindled and that problems may be talked through and thought through with openness and reason. And if one form of loving relationship dies, may another be born from the ashes of the old without bitterness and recrimination.

We pray for all who are bearing the pain of a broken relationship and finding the sense of loss difficult to cope with. We pray for those who have lost a close loved one in death. We pray that they may know that love is stronger than death, and that your everlasting love ensures the safety of their loved one and the assurance of their reunion.

'GOD IS LOVE, and those who love are God's friends and God is their friend.'

We pray for those whose love is for someone of their own sex. For gay couples and friends as they seek to express and develop their love in a society which can still be hostile, persecuting and ridiculing, even excluding them from the celebrations of Valentine's Day.

We pray for the Church which has yet to heed the advice of Jesus, 'Do not judge, or you will be judged.' We pray for Christians who are still reluctant to accept and embrace, as Jesus did, those the world rejects.

We pray that gay people may come to know that their love, like all love, comes from you, and that they may receive courage as they look in hope for a kinder, gentler world.

'There is nothing to fear in love. Lovers overcome their shyness and nerves. Fear has to do with feelings of guilt. You don't really love until those feelings have gone.'

We pray for those who find it difficult to love. We pray for those who received little affection as children and so find it difficult to give affection. We pray for those who have been abused and harshly treated by those who have loved them. For victims of rape, and for the rapist.

We pray for those who are shy and lacking in confidence. For those who must first learn to love themselves before they can love others. We pray for those who on the whole prefer to be alone, but nevertheless need the assurance that they are loved and cared for.

We pray that we may all show our love by respecting the differing needs and wishes of individuals. May we, your people, learn to put your greatest commandments before all other considerations.

'God has made it clear what is expected of us. Those who love God must love all members of the human family.'

Ash Wednesday Prayer

Loving God, you care for everything and everybody; you take us as we are and give us the means to improve. We want to shake off the bad that has such a hold on us. We want to be at ease with you and at ease with ourselves.

You understand our problems; you have lived our life in the person of Jesus, the sign of your love. Through him we know you and get your help.

Amen (Or 'Yes')

1st Sunday in Lent

Jesus, you went without food for six weeks; then you proclaimed the New World Banquet, and invited your friends to party.
Help us learn your way of dealing with evil, to live positively and cheerfully.
Amen (Or 'Yes')

Family Sunday

(Mothering Sunday)

Jesus, you experienced family life, its advantages and its restrictions. You loved children and sat them on your knee. You also welcomed those whose families were broken and children who were disadvantaged.

Share with us your breadth of vision and the inclusiveness of your love. Help us to love our natural families and to get on with them; and help us to extend our families to include others who look to us for love and care.

We remember with gratitude those who cared for us in our earliest days, and we accept our responsibility look after the young and the old especially, and to treat others even better than we have been treated, as their needs require. Help us to be the family you would wish to be a member of.

Amen (Or 'So be it')

The Jesus Prayer

Alternative variations:-

1. Jesus, God's Likeness, fill me (us)* with your love.
2. Jesus, God's Chosen, help me in my weakness.
3. Jesus, friend of the friendless, be my friend.
4. Jesus, Bread of Life, feed me now and forever.
5. Jesus, True Vine, keep me close to you.
6. Jesus, Word of God, teach me your truth.
7. Jesus, Way, Truth, Life, help me to decide.
8. Jesus, God's Lamb, take my guilt away,
9. Jesus, my Leader, keep my eyes on you.
10. Jesus, Divine Host, get me to relax.
11. Jesus, full of fun, make me laugh.
12. Jesus, Divine Guest, come into my heart.
* and elsewhere.

(Make up your own, using the same pattern.)

Passion Sunday

Jesus, you shared our humanity to the full, including our
suffering. You suffered not only the torture chamber and brutal
execution with their humiliation and intense pain, but the
suffering of bereavement, rejection and betrayal.

You suffered agonies of fear and doubt, loneliness and misun-
derstanding. Totally vulnerable, you surrendered control, and
even experienced the feeling of separation from God.

Help us in our times of suffering to trust in your nearness and
your complete understanding. Share with us your composure,
your patience and resilience. Revive our hope and confidence so
that we may be open to share your joy.

Amen.

Palm Sunday

Jesus, just once, you encouraged your people to let go, to parade and sing and shout slogans in your support. You allowed children to break free and annoy their elders, to pat the donkey and climb the trees and tear down branches.

Help us to catch the spirit of that day, to know that it is right sometimes to let go, perhaps in preparation for more serious times.

Hosanna, freedom now, let God's New World come.

Son of brave and cultured David, sensitive and versatile, loyal and loving friend, we cheer you, we hug you, we give you the spotlight.

Yes, Yes, Yes.

Good Friday

Dear Loving God, we call to mind the worst of days and the best of days; the day when all the evil and hatred in humanity conspired to put you on the cross, to suffer the worst of pain and indignity and to die; the day when the course of history was changed, when your love was shown, naked and beautiful and vulnerable; when the world was shown a new way to reach its goals and bring about happiness and peace; the day the universe rocked on its hinges, powers and authorities were shaken, hearts were opened, all forgiven; a day of darkness and mystery, secret and private within your being, and a day when all are welcomed into the most intimate friendship possible with you. The only way we can express what happened on Skull Hill that day is with deep silence.

(Long period of silence.)

The Stations of the Resurrection

1. The Roman Soldiers Guard the Grave
Jesus, soldiers watched at your grave: we pray for all who
watch: soldiers, police, security guards; those who attend the
sick, those who await the result of operations, those who watch
over the dying.
Patient Jesus...*Watch with them*

2. Jesus rises
Silently, with no one watching, Jesus leaves the tomb: we pray
for all recovering from illnesses, for those struggling out of
breakdowns, for those about to go through death, the greatest
recovery of all.
Rising Jesus....*Keep them company*

3. Mark sits on the tombstone
Mark sits on the tombstone and becomes an angel, ready to
announce the good news: we pray for those who speak the
message of life and hope and resurrection; that they may be
heard and understood and believed.
Good News Jesus...*Excite the fearful and doubting*

4. The women meet Jesus
The women disciples meet with Jesus and greet him warmly:
we pray for all women institutionally humiliated by their
church or religion, that they may have the courage, shrewdness
and patience to outwit their oppressors.
Jesus champion of women...*let all share your true respect for them*

5. Rocky and Larry inspect the grave
Rocky and Larry inspect the tomb, they are confronted by a

mystery, Rocky is impatient, Larry afraid since he has been in such a tomb himself: we pray for a greater sense of mystery in the presence of life and death, less fear and greater hope; we pray for all who are bewildered or confused today.

Jesus, hero in life and death...*help us enjoy life and face death with expectation*

6. Great hearted Mary and the Gardener

Greathearted Mary, grieving for her man, meets the gardener near the tomb. He greets her by name and she realizes that Jesus is not dead, but embodied wherever there is life and beauty.

Jesus, alive forever...*help us to recognize you here and now*

7. Clover and his Partner

Clover and his partner meet with a traveller on the road and invite him home to stay. As the bread is broken they see Jesus.

Jesus, on our journeys, at our tables...*open our eyes to see you*

8. The Friends in the Function Room Upstairs

The door is locked, but you are not locked out. Suddenly you are there. You are wounded, but bring calm.

Jesus, not bound by time or space...*we break our chains*

9. Twin

Twin needs more proof; he wants to examine and touch. Lovingly you let him have his way. He is convinced.

Jesus, meet us at the point of our doubts...*and arouse our trust*

10. The Sea Shore

A stranger greets some fisherfolk and helps them at their work. They gather round for a barbecue and sing songs of happiness.

Jesus, when we include...*we include you*

Easter

So you have risen from the dead, dear Jesus. Of course you
have. What could be more natural! What could hold such love?
If there is any reason in the multiverse of universes, this is it.
Otherwise nothing makes sense.

We celebrate the died and restored to live; we welcome sadness
turned into joy, despair into hope, the most depressing of all
ends into the most hilarious of beginnings.

You live in our hearts and minds. But much more, you are alive
everywhere, in everything, in everyone. As those who rejoice
we proclaim, to those who still mourn we shout aloud:-

(Solo Voice) Jesus has risen!

(All) **He has risen indeed!**

Ascension

Must we abuse you, Jesus, first citizen of heaven, with talk of power and majesty? You are the humble one who does not expect credit thereby.

Pardon us for entering you in our competitive races, when you seek as ever to love and to serve. In our pride we have exalted you from us and set you apart. You have said, 'I am with you always.'

You are at one, as ever, with our weaknesses, our struggles, and our mistakes. The cloud has parted you, the glory cloud of our own making. Yours is the presence of God that takes us up with you and into you.

It is your full ascending we would celebrate, the ascension that leaves no one behind. You seemed to leave in quietness; when we are quiet we shall know you are here.

So be it.

Pentecost

Spirit of God, feminine, creating, enabling, comforting,
cuddling, enthusing, inspiring:
Challenge and soften our masculinity, so that we may reap your
crops of love, joy and peace.
Be known to us everywhere, rush like the wind, knock down
our fences and suck away our dust, blow us off track.
Open us to your truth and lighten us up with patience and
kindness.
You cause everything to move. Keep us moving with you.
Yes!

Trinity

God of love, expressed in community, we seek to understand you in a model you have presented to us. You are One and more than one.

We experience you as Parent, combining the very best of mother and father;

You are the human portrait of yourself, the man Jesus, our eternal friend;

You are the Spirit, she who is the giver and sharer of life.

Can you be much more? You are infinite, with endless possibilities. Always the same, always different, the one who always has been and is always new.

We know you as Trinity. Help us not to confine you or reduce you to a formula. Full and loving God, we adore you and give ourselves to you.

Morning Prayer

Loving God, you have brought us to the beginning of a new day. Help us to remember you from time to time, so that we may be aware of your presence always.

Keep us from harm and danger, unless we need to go through them. Help us to help someone else today and to restrain ourselves from causing grief to anyone.

Help us to be happy, so that we may help others to be happy too.

Amen (or 'Yes')

Evening Prayer

Light up our darkness, dear loving God, and in your great
kindness defend us from all that we are frightened of.
We take love's risks and share love's joy, travelling life's road
with Jesus, our Saviour.
Amen.

Hebrew Grace

Grace before meals and before sharing bread and wine.

Food
'Thank you, our God, ruler of all that is. From the soil you have produced crops of grain for our hands to make into tasty bread. We know your constant goodness and pledge our loyalty to you.'
So be it.

Drink
'Thank you, our God, ruler of all that is. In our orchards and vineyards you have made fruit to grow for us to make into pleasant drinks. We know your everlasting love and bring our love to you.'
Yes!

As I Am

Loving God
Thank you for making me as I am;
Thank you for accepting me as I am;
Thank you for using me as I am;
Thank you for loving me as I am.
Yes!

Launching Pad (Sursum Corda)

V. Prepare yourselves in mind and mood!

C. *We are ready to meet with God!*

V. It's time to show our thanks to God!

C. *The right response to love is love.*

V. Love is the only response, and wherever we are, and in whatever mood, we should show our love for you, Father, Mother, Friend.

A. *So, with those who have done it before and with those who are doing it now, lovingly we thank you and welcome you among us.*

Good, wise and beautiful is the Lover of Millions. Life and love is proof of your presence. God above praise, we celebrate because of you.

Now It's Time

At Easter Breakfast Communion.

Now it's time, it's breakfast time:
Try some cereal or toast,
Healthy fruit or hot cross buns;
Thanks to God who is our host!
Rolls with honey, jam or spread,
Tea or coffee brings a 'Wow',
Then we'll share wine, fish and bread,
That will show God with us now, (now, now, now...)
(Simon Walkling 2008. Tune: Doh a deer –'The Sound of Music')

Celebrating a Friendship

Scripture Sentence. *'Dear friends, let's love one another, because love is a present from God. Everyone who loves shares a family likeness with God and has a relationship with God. Anyone who doesn't love doesn't have a relationship with God, because GOD IS LOVE...No one has ever penetrated the mystery of God's being. But if we love one another, God is part of us. God's loving nature can be seen in our loving.'* (1 Jn.4:7-8 & 12 ONE – 'The Call to Love')

Declaration of Intent. We are here today to affirm that the love that has brought Sadie and Diane together is from God, and to acknowledge God's approval of them as they live in company with each other. We also want to give them our support as their friends and to seek their good, now in our prayers, and in our future care and concern.

Prayer. *Extempore* or:- Loving God, today we celebrate your greatest gift, your gift of love. It is the gift of yourself, for you are love. You gave yourself to us in Jesus, and now you have given yourself to us again in these two loving people. Your love is miracle. It turns selfish beings into those who care more for someone else than for themselves; it turns those who use others for their own ends into those who seek only another's good; it turns those who are fickle and unreliable into those who aim to be loyal and steadfast; it turns the cold-hearted into the warm, affectionate and generous. Let your love be real in us today; let it be the foundation of everything we are; let it hold firm, come what may. Help us, God, to love **you** in response to your love for us. In the name of Jesus.

*Hymn e.g. 'Great God, your love has called us here' Brian

49

Wren, 'We are one in the Spirit' Peter Scholtes)

Expressions of friendship and exchange of tokens (e.g. rings)
Each friend repeats after the leader of the service.
In the presence of God and all here today, I, Sadie, declare my love for you, Diane, and rejoice in God's approval of our friendship. I intend to love you, care for you, and consider you before my own needs, in good times and bad times; I will be pleased when you are happy and grieve when you suffer; I will share your interests and hopes for the future; I will try to understand you even when I don't agree with you; I will help you to be your true self – the person God wishes you to be. For all this I ask God's help, now and in the days to come. In the name of Jesus.

Exchanging of tokens.
May these rings (tokens) be a reminder to Sadie and Diane of the bond between them and a witness of their love for one another and God's love for them.
Friends say together.
We exchange these rings (tokens) as a mark of our friendship and our love.

Passing on the Goodness. God cheer you and look after you; God convince you that life is good; God assure you that love is the lasting reality; God satisfy your deepest needs; God give you peace, now and forever.

*Scripture Readings.
1 Samuel 18: 1b-4 and Ecclesiastes 4: 9-12
or Ruth 1: 1-18
1 Corinthians 13

*Address
*Prayers (See prayers for Valentine's/ Dwynwen's Day)
The Pattern Prayer (*Those present repeat after the leader of the service*)
Loving God, here and everywhere, help us proclaim your values and bring in your New World. Supply us with our day to day needs. Forgive us for wounding you, while we forgive those who wound us. Give us courage to meet life's trials and deal with evil's power. We celebrate your New World, full of life and beauty, lasting forever.

*Hymn e.g. 'We pledge to one another' Jill Jenkins; 'I vow to you, my friends of earth' Jim Cotter – both to 'Thaxted'(Holst)
The Beauty. The Beauty of Jesus our Leader, the Love of God our Parent, and the Joy of the Spirit our Uniter be with us for ever.

* = *optional*. (*Note:* I composed this service sometime in the mid 1980s when I received a request from a gay couple for a service of blessing on their relationship. I explained that since God's blessing was already received in the love they had for one another there was no need of a blessing from me, but that I would gladly celebrate with them in the presence of God and their friends. This order, though suitable for gay relationships, is suitable for any two friends wishing to proclaim and celebrate their relationship, whether it be sexual or non-sexual, including heterosexual partners who do not want the pressure and expense associated with the customary religious and legal arrangements. I have joyfully used the service on many occasions.)

THIS IS TO CERTIFY

That .... **and** ....

declared their love for one another in the presence of God and witnesses, and expressed their intention to enjoy life in each others' company and to care for one another as long as life lasts.

Venue...

Date...

President at Ceremony...

'GOD IS LOVE, and those who love are God's friends and God is their friend.'
(1 John 4:16 'Good As New')

Song One

(Psalm 1)
Splendid are folk who never copy
Those who trash another's creed,
Thinking only of themselves,
Making fun of others' need.

Splendid those who honour God
And night and day think on God's love;
Their lives are green like leafy plants
That grow beside the river banks.

Like trees they offer tasty fruit,
And shade for those who feel the sun;
They guarantee the planet's health,
Sustaining life for everyone.

The selfish have such trivial aims,
Their cravings wander with the wind;
Their lives will fail the test of time,
Unlike the lives of those they scorn.

The caring know the help of God,
The selfish live and die alone.

Song 19 - Look above you

Look above you and see God the Artist:
Look around and mark God's hand:
Each day's search reveals something different:
Scan the night sky and understand.

In depths of quiet,
Silence unbroken,
Heard the world over,
God has spoken.

Like a bride on her wedding day,
The sun steps out at dawn;
Cheerily jogging a world-wide course,
Like an athlete training for the marathon.

In much the same way,
Bringing us cheer,
God speaks every day,
Making things clear.

The parts that clever talk can't reach
To drive away those moody blues,
God's eloquence can deftly sweep,
With undisguised good news.

Respect for God is a solid base:
Sound is God's Advice;
What money buys won't last as long,
Nor feelings sweet and nice.

Sometimes God a warning gives,
And sometimes speaks of a reward.
But we think we know better,
And hope to hide our faults from God.

I am your assistant, God,
So help me keep in check my pride;
Otherwise, that day will come
When I do something very bad.

May what I say and what I think
Be just as you would have;
You are my Leader and my Strength,
My Freedom and my Love.

Song 22

(L) My God, my God, why have you left me
All day long in pain to groan?
Will you leave me alone in misery?
Even at night no sleep will come.

(C) You're a celebrity,
Praised by our people -
The one the old folk trusted
And were never disappointed.
When *they* cried out you promptly came,
Their faith was not once put to shame!

(L) But I'm a parasitic worm,
Mocked by low, despised by high;
Each one makes a joke in turn,
And pulls a face when passing by.

(C) 'Get God to do something;
Don't put up with it;
Haven't you told us
You're God's favourite?!'

(L) I can count my bones - I am so thin.
The heartless spit, or stare at best
To see the sorry state I'm in;
While greedy gamble for my vest!

(C) God, without you I'm so afraid,
Come back quickly to my aid.

(L) My soul is in a desert place
Surrounded by ferocious beasts;
Towards me rush stampeding bulls -
(PAUSE)

And then – THE NIGHTMARE CEASED!!!

(C) So God was with me all the time,
God saw my pain and heard me call,
Despite what pious preachers say,
GOD NEVER TURNED AWAY AT ALL!

(L) So, this is clear – all those who die,
Decompose, or burn to dust,
Will, like me, again serve God.
This is a word that you can trust.

(ALL) The word will sound in future days,
The Saviour for the years to come;
Each newborn baby joins the praise
And learns to tell what God has done.

Song 23 - Just like a shepherd

Just like a shepherd in olden times
My leader shows the way,
And finds the shady spots to rest,
Where quiet waters play.

My spirits lift in such company;
I find the strength to walk
The paths of justice and of peace,
Even though the cynics mock.

I'll even count my life's breath cheap
And face that dark ravine;
I'll follow still the steady staff
And tread the way it's been.

The table's set to celebrate:
The enemy's looking glum.
With pleasing touch and healing scents
Are served the food and wine.

There's not a lot that can go wrong
Since in God's love I stay;
With present friends and those to come
I'll venture, rest and play.

Song 32

It's great to know you've been forgiven
And your mistakes forgotten;
It's great to be sure
God's not keeping a score;
That would be truly rotten!

I was so very, very ill,
Losing strength, confined to bed
I thought that you were hurting me,
I was confused in heart and head.

Then I saw where I'd gone wrong,
And told you all about it,
I said, 'I'm really sorry God',
And you just said, 'Forget it!'

So I fully recommend
When you're up to the neck in it,
Have a good long talk with God,
You will not regret it.

Sometimes a cozy corner God,
Shielding me from trouble;
Sometimes the one who leads the cheers
When I have won a battle.

I have experience to share,
To stop folk going wrong;
Let me keep an eye on you,
And you won't come to harm.

Don't be like a horse or mule
Not yet fully trained;
Watch that temper and those moods,
Friendships can be strained.

Those who go out to do wrong,
For themselves make punishment;
Those who trust their lives to God
Nestle in Love's arms content.

So cheer up, give thanks to God,
You who seek the best;
Sing and shout and celebrate,
In God's goodness rest.

Song 118

Say 'Thank you' to God - always good, love that never gives up!

Come on, God's people, SAY IT -
'God's love never gives up!'

You members of the clergy, say it,
'God's love never gives up!'

All those who have reverence for God, say it,
'God's love never gives up!'

I was in a bad way when I asked God to help;
God answered, bringing me back to reality.
God is beside me at this very moment
And I'm no longer afraid;
Nobody will get me down!

God is my source of strength;
I make light of my troubles.
It's much better to have God as your friend
Than anyone else you can think of;
God is a better standby than good connections.

I was made to feel inadequate by people who didn't understand me;
God helped me not to be put off by them.
I felt restricted, but God got me to relax.

It was like being surrounded by a swarm of bees,
Or trapped in a house on fire,

But God rescued me.
I was in free fall, but God's arms caught me.
God is all I need, my resources, my inspiration,
And now my new life.

Listen to the song being sung by God's friends:

'God acted superbly
And saved the day:
God is the victor;
We have a new future'

I'm not going to die after all -
I'm going to live to tell the story of what God has done.

God set me a test and helped me through it.
Now all life's doors are open;
Just watch me striding ahead with confidence.
God is the way forward, as all God's friends can tell you.

Thank you, God, for answering me,
For helping me back to full health.
I was rejected as a misfit.
Now I'm the key figure.

People are saying:

'God's given us such a big surprise,
We scarcely can believe our eyes.'

We are here today because of what God has done.
Let's celebrate and have a party.

Welcome, if you would like to be a friend of God too.
We give you our very best wishes.
There is only one God, the God who has lightened us up.
Let's make some bright decorations
And deck the place with flowers.

Thank you for being my God,
I will always speak well of you.

Come on, everybody, say 'thank you' to God
- always good, love that never gives up!

Song 121

Pilgrim (*looking distraught and scratching his head*) I've been wandering all over the mountains looking for help. No matter how hard I try I can't find a solution to my problems. I've come to see you here in God's house. Only God can help me, the one who made the universe and our home here on earth!

Adviser 1. (*Nodding wisely*) God won't let you fall. God is your best friend. God is always awake.

Adviser 2. (*Nodding her agreement*) God looks after every one of you. God never dozes or falls off to sleep.

Adviser 1. (*Raises open hand in blessing*) God will guard you; God is by your side to make sure you're O.K.

Adviser 2. (*Raises two hands to make her point*) Although you have to spend a lot of time in the open air, the sun will not give you sunstroke, and the moon won't drive you potty!

Adviser 1. (*Shaking hands with the pilgrim*) God will be with you in every kind of danger; you can depend on God.

Celebration.

49) Whether Dull or Colorful

Whether dull or colorful,
The outsize and the small,
Commonplace or wonderful,
God loves and cares for all.

The pine trees in the cold lands
The palm trees in the warm;
The cactus and the snowdrops,
The sunshine and the storm.

The rhubarb in the garden,
The potted plants we buy,
The rock pools by the seaside,
The white gulls floating high.

God loves the creepy crawlies
And things that bite and sting;
The spider with her lace work,
The snake with patterned skin.

The people who are moody,
And those brim full of fun;
The strong folk and the gentle,
God loves us every one.

Variety is God's purpose.
And difference is God's choice;
God made the soaring tenor
And deep contralto voice.

As well as eyes outside us,
We have some inside eyes,
So we can share God's vision
And mark each day's surprise.
(After 'All things bright and beautiful' C. F. Alexander 1818-95)

Buttons Polished

Celebration

Bring to God

Bring to God a load of presents;
Write 'With Thanks' and wrap with care;
- thanks for status, health, acceptance,
Benefits we have to share.
God is special, God is special,
Advertise it everywhere.

Think what God did for our comrades
In the days of history,
When in trouble, need, rejection,
Gave them hope and set them free.
God is special, God is special,
Sheer dependability.

We are certain as the weather,
Sun today, tomorrow rain:
This brief life, we, oh, so careless,
Undervalue, to our shame.
God is special, God is special,
Mourns our loss and takes our blame.

We possess the ideal parent-
Mother, father, all in one;
Gently from our worst restrains us,
Heartens with a warm 'well-done!'
God is special, God is special,

67

Always there and full of fun.

Help us all you others out there,
Celebrate the one we name.
You can come to our opinion
Of the love always the same.
God is special, God is special,
Delivers the good, deserves the fame.
(After HF Lyte. Best to tune Regent's Square.)

Good and Wise and Beautiful

Good and wise and beautiful, Lover of millions,
Early in the morning, we sing our songs to you;
Maker, Saviour, Spirit, with us and beyond us-
Three ways to know you; feel your loving too.

Good and wise and beautiful! Loved by all your people!
Many you have rescued from a life of misery;
They don't feel that saintly; few of them are angels;
But they will share your bright eternity.

Good and wise and beautiful! Sometimes you seem absent -
Play a game of hide-and-seek to test our loyalty;
Holy sense of humour, gently fooling with us,
Shaming our pride with your humility.

Good and wise and beautiful, Lover of millions,
Everything you do is noble, sensitive and true;
Parent, Friend, Adviser, in us and beside us;
Three ways to meet you; bring our worship too.

(John Henson, after 'Holy, holy, holy' Reginald Heber. Tune
Nicea)

Love Divine

Love divine, all loves excelling,
Joy of heaven, to earth come down,
Fix in us your humble dwelling,
All your loving tokens crown:
Jesus, you are all compassion,
Pure, unbounded love, you are,
Visit us with your salvation.
Our humanity's brightest star!

Breathe again your loving spirit
Into every troubled breast;
Leaving thoughts of wealth or merit,
Let us find your promised rest.
Take away our lust of winning,
First and last and centre be;
Goal of faith, as its beginning,
Set our hearts at liberty.

Come, great lover, to deliver,
Let us all your life receive;
You are always with us, never
Will you those you died for leave.
We would always you be thanking,
Work for you like those above,
Talk with you and praise unceasing,
Basking in that constant love.

Finish then your new creation
True and loyal may we be;
Ever, through your liberation,

Ready for eternity.
Changed from glory into glory,
As with you we walk life's ways,
Till we see you and adore you,
Lost in wonder, love and praise.
After Charles Wesley.

Say 'Thank You' Now to God

Say 'thank you' now to God,
With hearts and hands and voices,
For such amazing things
In which this world rejoices.
God's loving arms were known
In early days of care;
And countless gifts of love
Show they are always there.

Since this most generous God
Will all our lives be near us;
Let's culture joyful hearts,
And signs of peace to cheer us;
Then may we feel that hand
To guide us when perplexed,
And face whatever comes
In this world and the next.

All thanks to God who loves
Us evermore, and with it
To Jesus, leader, friend,
Who gives the loving Spirit;
The ever lively God
Whose praise we gladly sing,
With lives set free and new
As our thank-offering.

(After Martin Rinckart 1586-1649 & Catherine Winkworth 1827-78)

Walk Beside Me

Walk beside me, friend and lover,
Till we make that better land;
Strength and weakness match each other;
Hold me, firm and tender hand.

Spread the table, spread the table -
We will share a banquet grand!

Meet me at the spring of water
Pure and clean and sparkling too.
Dreams of cloud and fire and thunder
Vanish as I drink with you.

Fill the glasses, fill the glasses,
We will drink to love and joy.

When we reach that chilly river
Conquer my anxiety.
You are life, - and death's destroyer;
I will share your victory.

Keep me singing, keep me singing,
Now and to eternity.

(After William Williams Pantycelyn – Tune: Cwm Rhondda, John
Hughes, Pontypridd.)

Communion

Come, for everything's ready

Come, for everything's ready, all the tables are laid.
It's a free invitation, so don't be afraid.
There is food here in plenty and the choicest of wine,
and God's sent out the message, 'Come in now and dine'.

Come and join in the party,
Come from near and from far!
God would love you to be there,
whoever you are.

We are sometimes too busy with our worries and care,
with jobs and with houses, not a moment to spare.
Life slips by so quickly as year follows year,
And God keeps on calling, but we've no time to hear.

There are others God calls in their hunger and need,
but we keep them out with our self-serving greed.
We grab the top places and the best of the fare,
but the food will just choke us till we learn how to share.

So let's go for the real feast for ourselves and for all,
and let the world know of God's wide open call.
Go out on the highways and invite them all in,
till the house has been filled and the party can swing!
(Raymond Vincent, August 2007
Tune: Invitation [Sacred Songs & Solos 405])

Deck Yourselves

Deck yourselves with joy and gladness,
Leave the gloomy haunts of sadness;
Come into the daylight's splendour,
There with mirth your praises render;
Come to him whose love unbounded
Has this awesome banquet founded;
Source of life and power and being
Now to us a welcome giving.

Like the sun, our moods you brighten
And our puzzled minds enlighten;
All the senses intermingling,
You set hearts and voices singing.
In your company, our Lover,
Teach us how to love each other;
All in love by you included,
No one by our pride excluded.

Jesus, bread of life, our Saviour,
Here we eat as friends together,
By you to this table guided,
Food you have in love provided.
From this banquet overflowing,
Sign of love beyond all knowing,
Let us catch your party spirit
And your new life truly merit.

After Johann Frank 1618-77 (also translated by Catherine
Winkworth 1827-78 *Deck thyself my soul...*)

Jesus Invites Us All

Jesus invites us all
To come and gather round;
Here, for whoever wants a meal,
A welcome will be found.

Some simple food and drink
Will give the signs we need
To know our friend once died for us,
And now is risen indeed.

As here on earth, love spoke
In everything he did;
Love speaks again in broken crusts,
And as the cup is shared.

Each of us different from
The person sitting near, -
Jesus breaks all the barriers down
And overcomes our fear.

So now we lift our hearts,
Feelings and voices raise;
Jesus requests our company;
Let's shower him with praise!

(After Isaac Watts 'Jesus invites his saints' tune: Bod Alwyn)

Mae Gan Yr Iesu Gwadd

Mae gan yr Iesu gwadd -
Mae ganddo groeso mawr
I bawb sy'n fodlon, at ei fwrdd,
Beth bynnag bod eu gwawr.

Digon yw'r syml bwyd
I roi arwyddion mawr
O'r ffrind a threngodd droson ni
Wedi gyfodi nawr.

Pan oedd ef ar yr ddaear,
Cariad oedd yn ei lais;
Mae cariad yn siarad hyd yn hyn,
Yn y crawenau cras.

Gwahanol ydyw'r rhai
Sy'n eistedd gyda ni;
Mae Iesu'n torri'r ffiniau i lawr
A threchu ofnau i gyd.

Codwn ein lleisiau nawr,
Teimladau'n dod i lan;
Mae Iesu am ein cwmni ni -
Atebwn yn y fan.

This shall be my sign.

'This shall be my sign', said God,
'This shall be my sign -
I'll set my bow in the sky above,
So that all may know my love.
This shall be my sign.'

'This shall be my sign,' said God,
'This shall be my sign -
Cloud by day and fire by night;
All my ways are true and right.
This shall be my sign.'

'This shall be my sign,' said God,
'This shall be my sign -
His name shall be Immanuel,
God with us will ever dwell.
This shall be my sign.'

'This shall be my sign,' said God,
'This shall be my sign -
They'll put me up on a cross of wood,
Then I will be understood.
This shall be my sign.'

'This shall be my sign,' said God,
'This shall be my sign -
when you taste the bread and wine,
I am yours and you are mine.
This shall be my sign.'
(Words & tune by John Henson)

Christmas

As with Gladness Travellers Bold

As with gladness travellers bold
Saw a new star, pure as gold,
As with joy they caught its light,
Leading onward, beaming bright;
So, dear loving God may we,
On life's quest, your splendour see.

In our minds we see them come,
Jesus, to your lowly home;
There we watch them kneel before
 You, the one the true adore;
So may we find such a place
Where we glimpse your smiling face.

As they offered gifts most rare
At your lodging poor and bare,
So may we with holy glee,
Freed from pride and vanity,
All we value gladly bring
For your use, our friend and king.

Loving Jesus, every day
Keep us in your joyful way;
When our time on earth is past,
Bring us, travellers still, at last,
Where we need no star to guide,
Where no clouds your beauty hide.

In that heavenly country bright
We will need no other light;
You its light, its joy, its crown,
You the sun that goes not down.
There for ever, gone all tears,
We will worship with the Seers.
(After W.C. Dix 1837-98)

God's Messenger to Mary Came

God's messenger to Mary came one day,
He said, 'My name is Gabriel, okay?'
'I have surprising news for you -
I've called to say
You're going to have a baby -
Hooray, hooray, hooray!'

Some will cry 'shame' and turn their backs on you,
But you will gather friends both kind and true.
His origin's a mystery, but just for now;
A child for everybody!
That's the why and how!

Then Mary lost her fears and she replied,
'Whatever God thinks best I'm on God's side.
I'll sing a song of liberty and face the day.
I'm going to have a baby -
Hooray, hooray, hooray!'

Then Joseph did the decent thing - stood by;
'I'm going to be a Dad, so there, don't cry!
We'll travel down to Bethlehem,
There'll be less fuss.
Though many will be hostile,
This means 'God with us!'

So in the street outside the Inn Love came,
God's joy and peace to us in human frame;
And we can join the curious few who came to say,
'He is our little wonder!

Hooray, hooray, hooray!'

(After Sabine Baring-Gould 1834-1924)

Hark the Glad Sound

Hark the glad sound! The Saviour comes,
The Saviour promised long;
Let every heart prepare a throne,
And every voice a song.

He comes the prisoner to release
From fear and greed and shame,
Each prison wall that evil builds
Shall fall before his name.

He comes into a darkened world
To be its truth and light,
That those whose eyes are closed to God
May yet regain their sight.

He comes to bind the broken heart,
To comfort the distressed,
To pour the treasures of his grace
On outcast and oppressed.

Our glad hosannas, Prince of Peace,
Your coming shall proclaim;
And heaven's eternal arches ring
With your beloved name.

(Philip Doddridge 1702-51 altered.)

Hark, God's Merry Minstrels Sing

Hark, God's merry minstrels sing
Baby Jesus welcoming;
Peace to earth, heaven's kindly hand,
God's love in a bundle found.
Joyful, every land awake,
Your place at the party take,
Every colour kinship claim
With the child of Bethlehem.
Hark, God's merry minstrels sing,
Baby Jesus welcoming.

God eternally adored,
Jesus Christ, God's living Word;
Just in time we see him come,
In a humble craftsman's home.
Wrapped in flesh* God's present see,
Sign of love to you and me;
Pleased as one of us to dwell,
For he is 'Immanuel'.
Hark, God's merry minstrels sing,
Baby Jesus welcoming.

Greet the one who comes from far-
He the Magi's brightest star;
Greet the unwashed shepherd's friend,
Smiling love that knows no end.
He will seek no glory cheap;
He will sinners company keep;
Born to recondition earth,
Born to bring new hope to birth.

Hark , God's merry minstrels sing,
Baby Jesus welcoming.

(After Charles Wesley. *Here we re-introduce Wesley's original telling expression. For those who think the version they usually sing is the 'original', one only needs to say that Wesley began thus: 'Hark how all the welkin rings..')

He's Sharing a Bed

He's sharing a bed with
The camels and cows,
Young Jesus, our brother,
Locked out of the house;
The stars can be seen through
The gaps in the roof,
But Mary sits close by,
Her love is enough.

The baby wakes up
In the depths of the night;
His strong piercing voice
Gives the donkeys a fright;
There's no way of calming
Him – time for his feed;
So vigorous and healthy,
And Joseph so pleased,

In thought we are near you
In that outhouse tonight,
Though the cards that we send
Do not show it quite right;
We love you, dear Jesus,
And sad when you cry
In those children today
Who are too young to die.

So help us, our Saviour
To grow up with you,
Not dodging the conflict

Or blurring the view;
That feed-trough must lead us
To cross and to tomb;
For only 'Christ Risen'
Will scatter the gloom.

(After 'Away in a Manger' *Anon*)

It Came Upon a Midnight

It came upon a midnight clear
That lovely song of old,
From minstrels sent by God to sing
A message new and bold.
'All can know peace this very day,
On offer from above.
But you must seek the strangest place
To find God's gift of love.'

The minstrels have not gone away;
They still try to get through.
But we have sanctified their words
And dumbed their meaning too.
And 'silent night' and jingle bells'
Confuse in every store.
One scramble now while bargains last,
Buy more, and more and MORE!

Yes, greed and selfishness and strife
Have hogged the stage since then;
And after two millennia,
 We need to start again.
Turn down the volume, you may hear
The little baby cry.
Switch off the glaring blinding lights,
Stars still shine in the sky.

O please God, let the day come when
Your folk become aware
We cannot witness in your name

While honesty we fear.
Free us to speak in bold new ways,
Dismiss the old that's wrong,
And send the world Good News again,
Just like the minstrels' song.

(After E.H. Sears 1810-76)

Jesus Comes

Jesus comes with streamers flying,
Once as friend of outcasts killed;
Crowds of keen supporters with him,
Mouths with joyful laughter filled:
Loudly cheering (x3)
Ears and eyes and hearts are thrilled.

There's no mistaking this time round;
Perfect love now understood;
We who spat and sent him bound,
Broken, to a cross of wood,
Truly sorry (x3)
Glad that wrath is not his mood.

Dare we look or shyly glance
At that body full of grace?
Marks of thorns and nails and lance,
Sorrow lingering on his face?
Brightly smiling! (x3)
All our anxious fears give place.

Humble Jesus, same as ever,
Spurns a throne of grand design;
Loving always, judging never;
Towel and basin still the sign;
You will be with us (x3)
When we greet the end of time.

Merriment and quiet worship
Mingle as we work and wait;

For it is no tyrant lordship
We with dread anticipate;
Ours is the hurry (x3)
He'll be not a moment late.

(After Charles Wesley. Tune: Helmsley.)

Let All Mortal Flesh

Let all mortal flesh keep silence
lost in wonder at a child:
New born baby with potential,
seems so perfect, undefiled.
Though the weight of all the world hangs heavily,
'It's OK,' his father smiled.

Fragile flesh that knows its weakness
takes the challenges life brings.
Searching mind and working fingers,
open heart from which love springs.
Though the world can't see the God at work within,
with God's life creation sings.

Flesh and blood so bruised and broken
racked with pain upon the cross:
scorned, rejected, seems forsaken,
counted nothing more than dross.
Yet in Jesus' arms stretched out in selfless love,
God embraces pain and loss.

Born a poor child in a stable
challenging wealth's power to save.
Dying like a godless rebel
shows how violence can enslave.
Jesus shows God's chosen way of love,
ends the rule of pow'r in the grave.

Jesus then revealed as risen,
present here in symbols shared.

Bread and wine now speak of myst'ry,
love renewed and hope repaired.
In a world of climate change and bankruptcy,
God's way now in contrast declared.

After communion
So the wonder of a baby
after pain and strain of birth,
and the joy of resurrection
both affirm our human worth,
and the love of God that changes everything
is revealed on our patch of earth.

Christmas morning
In the darkness light is shining,
new hope can be seen with the dawn.
Share the good news with your neighbours,
celebrate that Jesus is born.
Make the link from Christmas through to Easter Day;
God's son wakes up with a yawn.

(Simon Walkling 2008)

Long Ago in David's Hometown

Long ago in David's hometown,
At the tavern, just outside,
Was a sturdy wooden hay box,
Where the horses would be tied.
Mary had her baby there;
Only Joseph seemed to care.

Then some women from their windows
Saw the young mum's dreadful plight,
Ran and formed a circle round her,
Brought provisions, set her right.
Mules and horses understood
They were sharing hay with God.

This young guy proved quite a scholar,
He was kind as he was bright;
Helping in the joiner's workshop,
Cooking by his mother's side.
And he gives us things to do.
Jesus, help us copy you.

Pattern for our human progress,
Mind and body, day by day;
Childhood instincts carried forward:
Childish follies cast away;
Learning how to feel for others,
Gaining sisters, adding brothers.

One day soon we shall be with him;
His great love invites us on;

Tavern, lakeside, skull hill, garden,
We will go where he has gone-
In the place he has prepared,
Love and laughter will be shared.

Not around a tinselled cradle,
Nor within a gaudy shrine;
Jesus sets our sights on new worlds,
Well beyond the trap of time.
Waiting till he calls us home-
So much work still to be done.

(After C.F. Alexander 1818-95)

O Come, All You Faithful

O Come, all you faithful,
Dancing and processing,
Raising your voices -
To Bethlehem.
Come with your trimmings,
Decorate the shelter,
O Come let us adore him (x3)
Beautiful boy.

True God of true God,
Light of light eternal,
Jumping for joy in a teenage womb;
Ground of all being,
Tiny toes and fingers. *O Come...etc.*

Here come the farmers,
Up the hill to Bethlehem,
Sheep left in fields below,
Wolves keep away;
Wild beasts and docile
By God's presence guarded. *O Come...etc.*

Eastwards in Persia,
Shamans meet to travel,
Sacks full of golden coins, sweet scents and balm;
Two years more searching,
 They will meet their Bright Star. *O Come...etc*

Sing merry minstrels,
Lead the celebration,

This world and worlds unknown join in the songs:
God's Christmas party
Is for everybody! *O Come...etc*

Jesus we greet you,
On your birthday morning,
We give our presents, you bring us joy;
God's life appearing
In a little body. *O Come...etc.*
(trad)

Some Were Warm

Some were warm and some were not
When, all snug in feeding trough,
Smiled with wind a baby brown,
Jesus, born in David's Town.

Chorus:
Welcome, very special day;
All our cares seem less some way;
Sing from Neath* to Kazakhstan,
God is found in Bethlehem.

'Say, you smelly shepherds low,
Why are you excited so?
Why have you left sheep and lamb
In the fields, exposed to harm?

'As we watched at dead of night,
Wandering minstrels caused us fright;
But they brought Good News in song,
Told us we should haste along.'

Two years later sorcerers came,
With a message much the same;
They looked quite peculiar,
Had been following a star!

Weird and unwashed join to praise,
On this merriest of days,
One who came for people all,
Not just the respectable.

* Or 'Sing from Maine, Slough, Stoke, Cork, Mull, Devon to...etc.'

(After Edward Caswell 1814-78 'See amid the winter's snow'.)

Today we welcome gladly

Today we welcome gladly, baby boy, baby boy,
True descendant of King David, - baby boy;
God who has friends without number,
From Abraham to Anna,
And died to be our Saviour, - baby boy, baby boy,
Feeding snugly from his mother, baby boy.

Ezekiel's 'Living Water', at her breast, at her breast,
And Daniel's 'Ideal Human' at her breast.
The new hope given to Sarah,
And Isaiah's promised Ruler,
The First One and the Last One, at her breast, at her breast,
For whom the choirs are singing, - at her breast.

He took no airs or graces - of his choice, of his choice,
And opened up his heart, of his choice;
He bowed his wounded head
While in love he ached and bled;
Now, he's risen from the dead - of his choice, of his choice,
To take away our dread, - of his choice.

So come, the good and bad, just as you are, as you are,
To receive the gift of 'Life', as you are;
Come quickly to the spring
Of every worthwhile thing;
With the Star-folk presents bring, as you are, as you are;
And with the choirs sing, as you are.

(Update/translation of the Welsh carol 'Ar gyfer heddiw'r bore'.)

We Are Freaks

We are freaks who follow the stars,
Pleiades, Neptune, Venus and Mars;
Men and women, dressed in linen,
Peddling our lucky charms....O

We have seen a bright new star,
Traced its track and travelled far;
From the East we've journeyed westwards -
Seeking out a baby rare!

We bring gold, a currency true,
All our wealth we offer to you;
Born in need, you have no greed,
But offer us values new......O

We have incense, sparking red,
Used by us to summon the dead;
Young life new, you bring life true,
Just as Zoroaster said.......O

We are healers of a sort,
Myrrh we use as last resort;
Ease our pain, remove the strain,
Sure healer of mind and heart.....O

You are brighter than a star,
Swarthy skin with smile so fair;
From the edge we make our pledge,
'You'll find us waiting there'.....O
(Correction of 'We Three Kings', - 'traditional misinformation')

You come again, Immanuel

You come again, Immanuel
As once you came to Israel.
When exiled far in Babylon,
You spread the path that led them home.

Rejoice, rejoice,
Immanuel comes once again
More joyful news to tell.

You come again, Immanuel:
You came to kind Rebecca by the well,
Waking her love for Isaac unseen,
Fulfilling thus old Abraham's dream

You come again, Immanuel.
You came to Joseph in his prison cell;
You set him up at Pharaoh's right hand,
To banish hunger from the land.

You come again, Immanuel:
When David to his friend bade farewell,
And Jonathan shed tears of woe,
You kept their youthful love aglow.

You come again, Immanuel,
As, in fear's grip, Elijah turned pale.
You spoke not in the wind or the fire,
But in the whispers of his heart's desire.

You come again, Immanuel

As when you came to Mary in the stall,
Wrapped in a parcel full of joy.
'Today to us is born a boy'.

(After the traditional eighteenth century advent hymn which
appears in many versions.)

Lent & Easter

All For Jesus

All for Jesus, all for Jesus!
Round the world our cheers shall speed;
For you are our hope and Saviour,
Source of joy and friend in need.

All for Jesus! You have shown us
Love while being crucified,
All for Jesus! Always with us,
Ever living, man who died.

All for Jesus! You will help us
Be your hands and voice each hour;
Nothing able to divide us,
Life or death or any power.

All for Jesus! In communion,
At the table you preside;
There we meet you, full life giver,
Then we venture, side by side.

All for Jesus! All for Jesus!
This our song shall ever be,
Till at last not one excluded,
All are welcome, loved and free.

After John Sparrow-Simpson (1859-1952)

Away with Gloom

Away with gloom, away with doubt,
With all God's folk we celebrate;
With all the morning stars we shout
The raising of our Mate;
Give him welcome, give Him welcome,
God's Likeness is our Mate.

Away with death and welcome life,
Like him we gain new life today;
And welcome peace, away with strife,
For love is here to stay;
Give him welcome, give him welcome,
God's love is here to stay.

Then welcome new day, sunrise grand,
With beauty old and beauty young;
By every group and every band
Let songs of joy be sung;
Give him welcome, give him welcome,
Let Jesus' fame be sung!

(After Edward Shillito 1872-1941 tune: Blairgowrie)

Pentecost

Dear Spirit of God

Dear Spirit of God, our hearts inspire,
And warm and light them with your fire;
Of you we drink, our fervor lifts;
You shower us with such precious gifts.

When sick, with healing balm you soothe;
You make our weary muscles move;
And as we grope to find our way,
You shine a torch as bright as day.

Blow fierce strong wind, knock barriers down;
Relax the good with singer and clown;
Then gentle, female dove proclaim
That peace which seasoned lovers claim.

Escort us to the home of God;
There show us how you play your part;
You Son and Father interface
And complement with mother's grace.

(doxology) Praise life and love and power and voice,
Beauty and feeling, thought and choice.

(Veni Creator Spiritus)

Easter

Fresh As Morning

Fresh as morning, sure as sunrise
See that God's love does not die.
Early morning on the Sunday,
See that Jesus will not lie.
Through the darkness of the Friday,
Through the Temple curtain torn,
Jesus makes his way to new life,
Waking those with sorrow worn.

Fresh as morning, sure as sunrise
See that God's love does not die.
To disciples lost and lonely,
Jesus comes to those who cry;
With our names that he speaks gently,
With the word to tell our friends,
Jesus calls us to a new life:
Love and hope that never ends.

Fresh as morning, sure as sunrise
See that God's love does not die.
Giving people joy and purpose,
Jesus leads through low and high.
Bread that's broken, wine that's poured out,
Life laid down and life restored;
Jesus shares with us his new life;
Stretched and challenged, never bored!!!

Simon Walkling 2007 (Tune: 'Migaldi, Magaldi' – Welsh traditional)

Go to dark Gethsemane

Go to dark Gethsemane
You who face decision's hour;
There you will your Leader see
Torn between his love and power:
Do not shun the sweat and tears;
Share with God your hurt and fears.

Follow to the judgement hall;
See an honest man on trial;
Watch him face accusers, all
Filled with jealousy and bile.
For us Jesus takes the cup -
Drinks the bitter mixture up.

Time to climb the skull-shaped rock,
Scene of many a cry of pain;
Righteous hiss and hoodlums mock
Majesty exposed to shame.
'Father spare them,' hear him pray,
As you turn your eyes away.

Look, the sun comes out again,
And there's springtime in the air;
Listen to the buntings sing
In the olives here and there.
Even in Gethsemane
Life and Love go dancing, free.

(After James Montgomery 1771-1854)

He Is Alive

He is alive! Time to rejoice;
Now is the day to find your voice:
Tell every culture, every creed,
'The one you seek is risen indeed!'

He is alive! Who then shall fear
To face life's challenges and care?
Or make their feelings truly known
To him who craves no crown or throne?

He is alive! The verdict stands-
You are set free by nail pierced hands;
Justice more kind than courts decide,
- a judge who takes the offender's side!

He is alive! The barriers fall;
The Holy City welcomes all;
Villains and victims, straight and queer,
All now to one another dear.

One world – a dream beyond all hope
Jesus has brought within our scope;
You know his love, you know his name,
So sing along and spread his fame!
(After Josiah Conder 1789-1855 'The Lord is King! Lift up thy
voice.' Tunes Niagara or Church Triumphant.)

Lent

Jesus, going without food

Jesus, going without food
In a rocky desert place,
Hot by day and cold by night,
Stared all evil in the face.

Hard it was for that young man,
With his famous appetite,
To forsake friends' company,
Swinging parties, laughter bright.

Scorpions sporting deadly tails,
Snakes in slithering twists and bends,
Lions and wolves with cruel fangs,
- Not the easiest of friends!

Great decisions to be made-
Power or service? Love or fame?
Flee the world or be its mate?
Lead revolt or heal the lame?

Who were those who came to care
For the Christ, exhausted, weak?
Lepers' commune? Desert friars?
They were angels, so to speak.

Praise to God; Give Jesus thanks
That he made the loving choice;
Sinners welcomed, fasts postponed,

Desert people find their voice.

(After 'Forty days and forty nights' G.H. Smyttan 1822-70
Best to tune 'Glad with Thee' Geoffrey Beaumont)

Good Friday

Lift high the cross

Lift high the cross, and Jesus' love proclaim
Till the whole earth rejoices at his name.

Mark, friends of Jesus, how your Leader trod,
The truest human, with the heart of God.

All who are followers of the crucified
Seek to display the love of him who died.

In harmony and rhythms bold they raise
From east to west their lively song of praise.

Jesus, once lifted, for all time to view,
As you have promised, draw us now to you.

All types included, lead your revellers past
the cross and empty graveyard, *'free at last!'*

(G. W. Kitchen 1827-1912 & M. R. Newbolt 1874-1956 altered once
again. Tune: Crucifer.)

Pentecost

Our Leader Jesus, when he breathed

Our Leader Jesus, when he breathed
His kind and warm goodbye,
A guide and source of strength supplied
With us to stay.

She came in tongues of living flame,
To teach, equip, enthuse;
All bracing as the wind she came,
With thrilling news.

She came, good influence to be,
A cheerful, helpful guest,
To set the minds imprisoned free
And bring them rest.

And hers that gentle voice we hear,
Soft as a summer breeze,
That checks each fault and calms each fear,
And eases grief.

And every virtue we possess
And every work inspired,
And every act of kindliness,
By her are fired.

Spirit of love and truthfulness,
Our dullness deal with now;
Our hearts would be a pleasant place,

To dance with you.

(After Henriette Auber 1773-1862)

Good Friday

There was in Old Jerusalem

There was in Old Jerusalem
A hill outside the wall,
Where Jesus died upon a cross
To show God's love for all.

We do not know, we cannot tell
What pain he had to bear,
But we believe it was for us
He hung and suffered there.

He died for each, he died for all,
The evil and the good;
One family of love to make,
United by his blood.

There was no heart so willing to
Forget how we had been;
He pointed to the open gate
Of heaven and led us in.

O dearly, dearly, has he loved!
We ought to love him too,
And trust him now to set us free
To build God's Bright World New.

(After Cecil Frances Alexander 1818-95)

Lent

Twists the Tornado

Twists the tornado over the lake;
Efforts in vain, they're bound to sink;
As for the captain, he's asleep,
Still and calm.

'Wake up, all's lost', in terror cry
the seasoned sailors, set to die;
Jesus stands tall, his voice raised high,
'Hush, keep calm!'

The wild wind drops, the angry sky
lightens, and waves rock lullaby;
The sweating oarsmen heave a sigh
At the calm.

When panic tries to make us slip,
Threatening to sink our leaky ship,
Steady us in your mighty grip,
Source of calm.

(After Godfrey Thring. 1823-1903. Tune St. Aelred in C minor.
**Amend first four notes of melody to ascending arpeggio:
middle C, Eb, G, upper C.)**

Good Friday

We Sing the Praise

We sing the praise of him who died,
One Friday on a Roman cross;
He is our Life, - the crucified:
Compared with Him all else is loss.

The cross! It takes our guilt away,
It holds the fainting spirit up;
It cheers with hope the gloomy day,
And sweetens every bitter cup.

Inscribed upon the cross we see,
In shining letters, 'God is love';
His arms are stretched upon the tree
To show us friendship from above.

Those arms! They call us to be brave
And put our trust in love, not might;
Their love is stronger than the grave,
They welcome to eternal light.

(Thomas Kelly 1769-1855 altered)

Lent

When mothers and fathers their children brought to Jesus

When mothers and fathers their children brought to Jesus,
His close companions, all polite,
Said, 'Come another day.'
But Jesus wasn't pleased at-all,
'My purpose is to welcome all.'
'Please bring them now, at once, here to me.'

For some were unmarried, and others separated,
And some were excommunicated, branded 'demonized'.
But Jesus wants his party full,
The po-faced and the silly fool;
'All, all are welcome to friendship with me.'

Oh! Some of the children were really rather dirty,
And some had runny noses, and
Their clothes were 'charity'.
But Jesus didn't seem to mind;
'Who's first for cuddles?' – smile so kind.
Dear loving Jesus, make your feelings ours.

So 'friends of the family' make sure you're on His wavelength;
Support, not judgement, be your aim -
Keep an unbiased mind.
Unless you imitate the child,
Accepting, trusting, open, mild,
God's New World show might just pass you by.

After (a long way after!) W.M. Hutchings, 1827-76 'When mothers of Salem'.

(Tune: Salem- German Students' Song)

Easter

Where Are You?

'Big Mary'
(Mary Magdala)

Where are you? Where are you
My healer and friend?
You seem very far, very distant?
Then you call me by my name,
And nothing is the same;
God with us, share love here today.
'Clover'
(Cleopas)
Where are you? Where are you
Companion and friend?
We said you're the one come to free us.
Then you meet us on the road
And help us bear our load;
God with us, share hope here today.
'Rocky'
(Peter)
Where are you? Where are you
My leader and friend?
I never meant to deny you.
Then you ask if I love you,
Point me to pastures new;
God with us, share joy here today.
'Twin'
(Thomas)
Where are you? Where are you

My teacher and friend?
I know I need some convincing,
But by staying with your friends,
I find life that never ends;
God with us, share faith here today.
Disciples, women and men
Where are you? Where are you
Our saviour and friend?
Behind bolted doors we are hidden.
Then your Spirit sends us out,
Despite our fear and doubt;
God with us, share peace here today.
God's people everywhere, in every day and age
Where are you? Where are you
Our friend and our God?
The world is in turmoil around us.
But now in bread and wine,
Suff'ring and hope combine;
God with us, share new life to day.

(Simon Walkling 2008. Tune: Ble'r ei di, yr hen 'deryn bach)

Good Friday

You there passing by

You there, passing by!
Come, see Jesus die!
He hangs on a cross
Silhouette to the sky;
Arms open above,
He shows you God's love:
What more can he suffer, your feelings to move?

He hangs there in state,
The object of hate,
The best of men sharing the criminal's fate.
Not only for the just
He dies on the cross,
But for those who abuse him or walk briskly past.

For you and for me
He speaks on that tree,
'Dear God, please forgive them and set their minds free.'
Love makes its appeal
And offers to heal,
But you can reject it, if that's how you feel.

And if you refuse?
His love you can't lose!
The permanent Friend you adore or misuse!
What's seen on this day
You can't sweep away,
He'll keep on inviting your love, come what may.

(After Charles Wesley)

Prayer

Amazing Grace

Amazing grace - how sweet the sound!
- that saw the worth in me;
Once feeling lost, and wandering round,
A New World now I see.

When ignorance ruled by fear in me
Then grace my fears removed;
How great that hour of setting free,
To know that I was loved!

In spite of many a foolish choice
I have survived thus far;
God's loving kindness had a voice
Or I would not be here.

Good things are what Love promised me
And I trust what Love says;
The God of grace my help will be
Now, and for all my days.

(After John Newton 1725-1807)

Come, Leader Dear

Come, Leader dear, and make your home
In every open mind and heart;
We seek your joy and peace to know
And in your New World play our part.

We need imagination's key,
The human touch, the lover's zeal;
Then we the contours of your love
Will know, though tongue can never tell.

Now may the God whose love extends
Beyond the grasp of any mind,
Be known in beauty recognized
In every type of humankind.

(After Isaac Watts 'Come dearest Lord..' v 3 may be used on its
own as a parting 'blessing')

Praise God

(Doxology)

Praise God from whom all goodness springs,
Rejoice in God all living things.
Give thanks God's people joined as one.
Praise Father, Spirit and the Son.

From You All Skill and Science Flow

From you all skill and science flow,
All feeling, care and love,
All calm and courage, faith and hope:
O pour them from above;
And part them, God, to each and all,
As everyone shall need,
To rise like flowers' scent to you,
In helpful thought and deed.

Bring quickly, God, that better day
When hate and violence cease;
And kinder rule fill all the world
With knowledge, health and peace;
When ever clean the atmosphere,
And fresher green the turf;
And our neglect destroy no more
Your garden here on earth.

Charles Kingsley 1819-75 (alt)
(Tune: Kingsfold)

God of Grace

God of grace and God of glory,
Pour on us your loving power;
Crown your ancient Church's story,
Bring its bud to glorious flower.
Grant us wisdom, grant us courage
For the facing of this hour.

See the hosts of evil round us
Scorn your Likeness, spurn his ways!
Fears and doubts too long have bound us;
Free our hearts to work and praise.
Grant us wisdom, grant us courage,
For the living of these days.

Heal your children's warring madness,
Bend our pride to your control;
Shame our wanton, selfish gladness,
Rich in things and poor in soul.
Grant us wisdom, grant us courage,
Or we'll miss your New World's goal.

Guide our feet to testing places,
Moved by love and motives true,
Challenging those gloomy faces
To the cause of freedoms new.
Grant us wisdom, grant us courage,
Failing not the world or you.

Save us from weak resignation
To the evils we deplore;

Let us prize your liberation,
Giving thanks for evermore.
Grant us wisdom, grant us courage,
So to serve you and adore.

H. E. Fosdick (1878-1969) alt.

Grace

(For meals. May be used at Communion)

Jesus, we join you at your board;
Be here and everywhere adored;
These good things share, and grant that we
Your banquet full may one day see.

Welsh Version

Iesu, ymunwn wrth y bwrdd;
Croeso i bawb, gyrwyd neb i ffwrdd;
Rhannu ein bwyd a diolch wnawn,
Yng ngobaith gweld dy wledd yn llawn.

(Tune: Rimington)

Jesus, I claim your promise

Jesus, I claim your promise
To hold me to the end;
It's good to know you're near me,
My leader and my friend;
I shall not fear life's challenge
With you right by my side,
Nor choose a crooked pathway
With you to be my guide.

I want to feel you near me,
So many choices here;
The worthless things that dazzle,
Slick voices in my ear.
The struggles deep inside me,
What knocks me all about
You give me heart to cope with,
Give purpose to my doubt.

I often hear you speaking
With gentle words and still
Above the noisy music
With which my head I fill;
Sometimes you make me hurry,
Sometimes you slow me down;
I know your smile's approval,
And recognize your frown.

You've cut some tracks before me
To open up the way;
The route is marked 'adventure', -

I'm starting from today.
Encourage and inspire me,
Strong love that has no end;
Prepare your famous welcome,
My leader and my friend.

(After J. E. Bode 1816-74)

We thank you, God, for using us

We thank you, God, for using us
For you to work and speak;
However trembling is the hand,
The voice however weak.

We bless you for each seed of truth
That we through you have sowed
Upon this hard and rocky soil,-
The living seed of God.

We thank you, gracious God, for acts
Of kindness there have been
From us, in any path of life,
Though silent and unseen.

For comfort volunteered perhaps
In days of grief and pain;
For words to troubled, weary folk,
Not spoken all in vain.

God, keep us moving on as in
Our keener days of old;
With love that opens arms to all,
Save us from growing cold.

Such honour, higher, truer far
Than quest for fame can find,
So to be joined, in work like this,
With you, our partner kind!
(After Horatius Bonar 1808-89)

My God I Thank You

My God, I thank you – You have made
the earth so bright,
So full of splendour and of joy,
beauty and light;
So many glorious things are here,
noble and right.

I thank you, God, that you have made
joy to abound;
So many gentle thoughts and deeds
circling us round,
That in the darkest spot of earth
some love is found.

I thank you, too that all our joy
is touched with pain;
That shadows fall on brightest hours,
that thorns remain;
So that earth's bliss may be our guide,
and not our chain.

I thank you, God, that though we are
so fully blest,
We never can, although we seek,
Be satisfied,
Until like Lazarus we sit
At Jesus' side.

(After Adelaide Anne Procter 1825-64)
(Tune: Wentworth.)

My Gracious Friend

My gracious Friend, you merit well
Each loving action I can show;
I own it as my greatest thrill
Your roles to play, your mind to know.

What is my being but for you,
It's sure support, its noblest end;
Your ever loving face in view,
Helping the cause of such a Friend.

I would not seek self-centred joy,
Or thrive against another's good;
Nor future days or powers employ
Spreading a famous name abroad.

It's for my Leader I would live,
The one who for my freedom died;
Nor could a world united give
More happiness than at his side.

His work my wrinkled age shall bless
When youthful vigour is no more.
And my last hour in life confess,
His love has animating power.

(After Philip Doddridge 1702-51 'My gracious Lord, I own thy right..')

My heart is resting

My heart is resting now, my God;
I will give thanks and sing;
My heart is at the secret source
Of every precious thing.
I thirst for springs of heavenly life,
And here all day they rise;
I seek the treasure of your love,
And close at hand it lies.

I have a heritage of joy
That now I cannot see;
The hand that bled to make it mine
Is keeping it for me:
And a new song is in my mouth,
To long-loved music set:-
Glory to you for all the grace
I have not tasted yet.

My heart is resting still, my God;
My life is in your care;
I hear the tunes of joy and health
Resounding everywhere.
'You are my choice, my everything',
With all your folk I say;
The music of our glad Amen
Will never die away.

Anna Laeticia Waring (altered). Ms. Waring was born in Neath in
1823, received her religious training from the Quakers, attended
Bethany Baptist Church in Cardiff, later joined the Anglicans and

became a famous hymn-writer. Her best known hymn is 'In heavenly love abiding', particularly popular in Wales. She died in 1910.

O God Of Love

O God of love, whose spirit wakes
In every human breast,
Whom love, and love alone, can know,
In whom all hearts find rest,
Help us to work for your New World
Till greed and hate shall cease,
And kindness dwell in human hearts,
And all the earth find peace.

O God of truth, whom science seeks
And reverent folk adore,
Who lights up every earnest mind
Of every clime and shore,
Dispel the gloom of error's night,
Of ignorance and fear,
Until true wisdom from above
Shall make life's pathway clear.

O God of beauty, oft revealed
In dreams of human art,
In speech that flows to melody,
In holiness of heart;
Teach us to mark all ugliness
That blinds our eyes to you
Till we express the loveliness
Of lives made free and true.

O God of righteousness and grace
To us in Jesus known,
Whose life and death reveal your face,

By whom your will was done,
Inspire your bringers of good news
To live the words they say,
Till you are known by everyone
And comes that lovely day.

(After 'O God of love whose spirit wakes' H.H. Tweedy 1868-1953
only slightly altered.)

We Thank You God for Using Us

We thank you, God, for using us
To work for you and speak;
However trembling is the hand,
The voice however weak.

We thank you for each seed of truth
That we through you have sowed
Upon this hard and stubborn earth, -
The living seed of God.

We thank you, loving God, for all
Of witness there has been
From us in any path of life,
Though silent and unseen.

For comfort ministered perhaps
In days of grief and pain;
For peace to troubled, weary souls,
Not spoken all in vain.

God, keep us still the same as in
Remembered days of old;
Please keep us learning how to love,
To warm the hearts grown cold.

Jesus to name, his love to tell
With voice unfaltering,
And face as bold and unashamed
As in our Christian spring.

O honour higher, truer far
Than earthly fame can send,
Thus to be used, in work like this,
So long, by such a friend!

(Horatius Bonar 1808-89. Lightly amended)

Your Way Be Mine

Your way be mine, dear God
Through dark and light and shade;
With you along the road,
I will be less afraid.

When feels the going rough
Coax me to still walk on;
Unnerved by challenge tough,
Prompt me to sing a song.

I cannot choose the cards
With which to play life's game-
I need your instinct large
To make the best of them.

The world you promised us,
So new, so bright, so fair,
I crave with hope and trust:
Help me to make it there.

Teach me to make my friends
In your surprising way,
Embracing those you send,
Uptight and tearaway.

And when I lose the plot,
Look's like there's no way through,
Remind me if I've not
Thought of consulting you.
(After Horatius Bonar 'Thy way not mine' Tune: St. Cecilia)

Message

And can it be?

And can it be that we should gain
Because the Saviour shed his blood?
Died he for those who caused his pain,
For those who him to death pursued?
Amazing love and can it be
That God should die for you and me?

'Tis mystery all! The immortal dies:
who can explore the strange design?
In vain the best of thinkers tries
To plumb the depths of love divine.
'Tis mystery all! Let earth adore,
And on new paths with God explore.

From timeless depths of space above,
The heart of God, with human face
Emptied himself of all but love,
And toiled for this wild restless race.
'Tis mercy all, for you and me;
He bled to set the whole world free!

Long our imprisoned senses lay
In evil's chains and darkest night;
Your visit came like sunshine's ray
To fill our prison cells with light;
Our chains fell off, and feeling new,
We walked into the day with you.

No awful judgement now we dread:
Jesus and all the world is ours;
We share his life, he is our head,
Each moment filled with loving powers;
Boldly we choose his upward way,
In love amazing day by day.

(After 'And can it be' Charles Wesley)

Begone, Unbelief

Begone, unbelief,
Our true Friend is near;
He offers relief,
Our conflict to share.
Though prayer feels like wrestling,
His cause cannot fail;
With Jesus in the cabin
We'll challenge the gale.

His love in times past
Forbids us to think
He'll leave us at last
In trouble to sink.
And can he have taught us
To trust in his name,
And thus far have brought us
To bring us to shame?

Although we complain
Of want or distress,
Frustration or pain,
He warned us no less.
If we would be like Him,
He made it quite clear,
Some hardship and testing
He expects us to bear.

How bitter the cup
No heart can conceive,
Which Jesus drank up

So others might live.
His way was much rougher
And darker it seems
Than we're like to suffer
In the worst of our dreams.

With Him, all we meet
Can be turned into good;
Some bitter, some sweet,
Makes a nourishing food.
Though downcast at present,
It will not be long;
A lasting contentment
Will brighten our song.

(After John Newton 1725-1807)

Come Christian Friends

Come, Christian friends there's plenty here for all to do;
God will supply the tools you need and give the know-how too.
With God the weak are strong, the over cautious dare.
Eagerly venture with a song and gladly burdens share!

Enjoy the Spirit's harvest - patience, joy and peace;
As you express and practice love, it surely will increase;
Loyalty, gentleness and generosity,
Kindness and self control - all serve to set the closed mind free.

Don't seek the bully's prize or power's security;
Don't sit with those who judge, or spread around guilt's misery;
Join with the victimized and be the outcast's friend;
Then you'll be one with Christ, tired and content at work day's
end.

(After Charles Wesley – 'Soldiers of Christ arise' Tune: 'From
strength to strength')

Come take your stand with Jesus

Come, take your stand with Jesus -
The bravest of the brave:
With him announce the Good News,
The power of love to save.
The virtues of the Spirit
You only have to ask:-
The patience and the kindness
To fit you for the task.

Come, take your stand with Jesus
To music of your choice;
Guitar or drum or organ
Will help you find your voice.
Right now a task awaits you
To match your best desire;
God will supply the wisdom
If you light up the fire.

Come, take your stand with Jesus
With labelled and condemned;
The righteous well may shun you
If you're the sinners' friend.
Fear not to haunt the venues
Where outcasts entertain;
We do not stand for Jesus
If we're their cause of pain.

For Splendid Folk

For splendid folk who have gone home to God.
Those who, on earth, life's pavements finely trod,
And whose example gladly we applaud,
Praise to their memory
While still we journey.

You taught them love, its way its truth, its life,
Jesus, God's Likeness, answer to earth's strife;
Reason their tool, replacing gun and knife,
Praise to their memory
While still we journey.

May we, like them, be in our thinking bold,
Leaving behind the patterns worn and old,
Drawn on by wisdom's gleam, not that of gold,
Praise to their memory
While still we journey.

The day will come when we with them unite,
All in new clothing, colours gay and bright;
Darkness at last defeated, only light,
Sharing our memories
Of all our journeys.

(After W.W.How 1823-97 'For all the Saints')

Gladly I Accept

Gladly I accept and humbly,
God is known in many ways;
Here on earth a man called Jesus
Showed us God with human face.

Hate was on the cross defeated,
Evil lost its power to cling;
Mighty love which won that victory
Is my guide in everything.

As each day the more I love him,
More upon my heart I take;
For themselves I cherish others –
Even more for his dear sake.

I with my unique experience
Meet his many other friends,
And we share not rule or dogma
But the love that never ends.

Great must be the appreciation
I can never give alone,
God the Spirit, God the human,
God the many and the One.

(After John Henry Newman 1801-90 tunes: Shipston or Sharon)

Glorious Things

Glorious things of you are spoken,
Longed-for New Jerusalem;
God, who came to us in Jesus,
Brings you down to earth from heaven;
Jesus is your sure foundation,
So you last through quake and tide;
Brightly sunlit, gates flung open,
Greeting guests from far and wide.

Like the cool streams from the mountains
We're refreshed by God's pure love.
We are called to spread God's banquet
And all fears of want remove.
We may faint, yet from this resource
Springs renewal at each stage;
All may change, but love works wonders
Without fail from age to age.

We give thanks for slave trades ended
At a date in history;
But today in many new ways
Slaves are bound more craftily;
Bodies sold and minds imprisoned,
Chained to tyrant creeds or things;
Still oppressed by work or boredom,
Money now no freedom brings.

Jesus, let me be a member
Of that city bright and fair;
Let me not be proud or grudging,

My new freedoms slow to share.
Free my mind and free my spirit,
Free my heart to serve and give;
Teach me that true freedom only
Comes as I help others live.

(After John Newton 1725-1807) Best sung to Bethany or
Blaenwern.

God Calls Us Into Partnership

God calls us into partnership
To plan a strategy
For a New World filled with life and joy,
An existence bold and free.
Nearer and nearer draws the time
Of the prophet's certainty,
When the earth will be filled with God's beauty and love
As the waters cover the sea.

Starting from here, right where we are,
The world our loving charge;
We stand with all those who are working for peace
And just causes, small and large.
'Join me and I will find you a job',
Jesus calls out to you and me-
'And we'll fill all the earth with God's beauty and love
As the waters cover the sea.'

The prophet's dream will soon come true
When we practice unity;
We need to find the love in our hearts
To embrace when we disagree.
Out with our hardness! Out with our pride!
Make room for charity!
Then the earth will be filled with God's beauty and love
As the waters cover the sea.

(After Arthur Campbell Ainger 1841-1919 'God is working his
purpose out')

God's Spirit Moves in Startling Ways

God's Spirit moves in startling ways
Her wonders to perform;
She navigates the mounting seas,
And rides our fiercest storm.

How subtly and how artfully
She twines her skills with ours;
Her genius, blended with our will,
Unleashes untold powers.

Don't be dismayed, you friends of God,
The future that you fear
Has nice surprises too, you'll see,
To fill your hearts with cheer.

Don't jump to quick conclusions, or
You may not read God right;
The picture of a grumpy God
Belongs to those in night.

God's plans stem from a heart of love,
As Jesus came to show;
Just see the flowers pushing through
From underneath the snow.

Please don't refuse to trust in one
Who wants the best for you;
Just give God of your space and time,
You'll get a clearer view.

(After 'God moves in a mysterious way' William Cooper 1731-1800)

How Light My Step

How light my step today,
So pleased I'm on my way
To where with God I feel most near.
Yes, you may find it odd
I think so much of God,
But no one's to my heart so dear.

It is the very place -
No matter what your face -
To meet in God's one family.
With steeple, tower or dome,
Or somewhere more like home,
I date with all humanity.

Once David did his dance,
Weird prophets spoke in trance,
And poets offered verses new;
Harps twanged and cymbals clashed
As choirs and priests processed
In purple, crimson, gold and blue.

Now we have finer fare,
Jesus, our friend, is there
Outmoding prophet, priest and king.
Wherever two or three
Meet for a cup of tea,
We know he will be sitting in.

I celebrate that place,
Though just a little space,

It is the point where all things join;
Only a step or two
For heaven to be in view
Where loving hearts abolish time.

And so I say to you,
You are my comrade true
Because we meet as friends of him.
We will his goodness share
With all who meet us there,
The place that counts outsiders in.

(After Isaac Watts 'How pleased and blest'- Psalm 122)

I Don't Know Why

I don't know why God's mighty love
To this world was made known;
Nor why to hard, ungrateful hearts
Such kindness has been shown.

But I've read the Jesus story-
Hope for the losers, cheer for the lonely;
I know that love's forever-
It will last beyond all time.

I don't know how God's Spirit moves
Directing love and life;
Nor why the world's so beautiful
Despite its pain and strife.

But I've felt her gentle thrilling
In music's rhythms and poet's meaning;
When any high endeavour
Transforms the gloom and grime.

I don't know what the future holds
Or how the end will come;
If God has more for me to do,
Or if my work is done.

But it's good to have a part in
God's work- creating, befriending, sharing.
I've seen His New World's colour,
And it's going to be fine!

(After 'I know not why God's wondrous grace' D.W. Whittle, 1840-1901)

It Passes Knowledge

It passes knowledge, that great love of yours,
Life-bringing Jesus, waiting at our doors;
Yet, of your love, in all its breadth and length,
Its height and depth, its everlasting strength,
We would know more.

It passes praises, heavenly love so true,
Attractive Jesus, winning us to you;
Yet, praise we love, so warm, so rich, so free,
That draws us, cold and selfish though we be,
Nearer to God.

It passes telling, your dear love, so strong,
Enabler Jesus, yet in speech and song
Our lips would speak to downcast far and near
Of love that can remove all guilty fear
and multiply.

But though we cannot sing or tell or trace
The boundaries of such love in our small space,
Our empty jugs again we trusting bring
To you who are of love the living spring,
For each to fill.

And Jesus, when your jolly face we see,
When some will dance and some will bow the knee,
We will your love, in all its breadth and length,
Its height and depth, with our united strength,
Together sing.
(After Mary Shekleton 1817-83 tune by Ira D. Sankey 1840-1908)

It's Very Rare

It's very rare to work for God,
To stand and take God's part
In this confusing, anxious world,
And not sometimes lose heart.

The God of Love plays hide and seek,
Or so it often seems;
God's New World frequently recedes
Way off beyond our dreams.

Playmates of God, just try again;
Search the unlikely spot;
Your dearest friend is teasing you,
Just waiting to be caught.

You'll be in luck when you have trained
Sharp instincts that can tell
That God is, like a summer breeze,
Warm though invisible.

It's hard to know what's right from wrong;
To question we are free;
To doubt is not disloyalty;
Love always has the key.

You're feeling down- you've joined the saints-
They know just how you feel.
Just rest awhile and shed your load;
The hidden one will heal.
(After F.W. Faber 1814-63)

Jesus has friends

Jesus has friends where'er the sun
Slow jogs its daily marathon;
His Good News spreads from shore to shore,
Confronting rich and aiding poor.

With him, at ease, can all converse,
Improve their best, control their worst;
His presence soothes the sharpest pain
And makes the old feel young again.

People and lands of every tongue
Enthuse him with their dance and song;
He mixes with the famous names
And joins the children at their games.

Right round the globe he sends his peace,
And prisoners joy at their release;
The weary find a welcome rest,
Their breaking hearts by him caressed.

If welcomed, he well-being brings,
Guilt and despair are banished things;
He forms a new humanity,
Freed from all pride and snobbery.

Let all things living join as one
And thrill to see his New World come;
No deep divides or barriers fast,
One family of love, at last.
After Isaac Watts – 'Jesus shall reign..'

For Our Friends

Jesus, we thank you for our friends,
Friends here on earth and in heaven too;
Our list of contacts never ends,
And we can always talk with you.

Our greatest friends are friends of yours;
They teach us, warn us and delight;
Whether our spirits droop or soar,
Their presence is a cheering sight.

The friends who leave us are not lost;
Whether they die or move away;
Closest the ones we love the most;
All yearning for reunion day.

You are the centre of our life,
Connected to your heart of love;
All feel the pain when there is strife,
Bliss when with unity we move.

We meet together day by day,
Each time your comradeship we crave;
Your spirit links us as we pray,
The very thought can heal and save.

The heavenly hosts around, above,
Provide us friendship without end;
And nothing bars us from your love,
Our closest and our dearest friend.

(After Richard Baxter 1615-91 'He wants not friends. Tune 'Angel's Song' Gibbons.)

Loved with Everlasting Love

Loved with everlasting love,
Led by grace that love to know;
Spirit, breathing from above,
You have taught me it is so.
O this full and inner peace!
O this gladness all divine!
In a love that cannot cease,
I am his, and he is mine.

Skies above are softer blue,
Earth around is sweeter green;
Something lives in every hue
That before I'd never seen:
Birds with happier songs o'erflow,
Flowers with deeper beauties shine,
Since I know, as now I know,
I am his and he is mine.

His for ever, only his:
No one shall us ever part!
Ah, with what such tender bliss
Jesus fills the loving heart!
Heaven and earth may fade and flee,
Light of sun in gloom decline;
Jesus lives eternally,
I am his, and he is mine.

George Wade Robinson 1838-77 alt.

One There Is

One there is above all others,
Well deserves the name of friend.
His is love beyond a mother's.
Costly, free and knows no end:
Those who once his kindness prove,
Find it everlasting love.

Which of all our friends to save us
Would have spent their life and blood?
On the cross he died to claim us
Friends of his and friends of God.
Super extra love indeed!
There in every hour of need!

When he lived on earth rejected,
'Friend of Outcasts' was his name;
Now above all praise exalted,
Yesterday, today, the same,
On the margins seeks his friends,
Duly to their cause attends.

We don't ease life for each other,
Yet he shares our load for us.
Day by day this friend and brother
Helps us without threat or fuss;
Though for good we give back ill,
Calls us sisters, brothers still.

Teach us how our moods to soften;
Show us, Jesus, how to care.

We, for shame, forget too often
You are with us everywhere;
One day, when we home are brought,
We shall love you as we ought.

(After John Newton 1725-1807 Tunes: All Saints or Gounod.)

Onward Christian Comrades*

Onward, Christian comrades*,
Jesus shows the way;
With his cross to guide us,
Love will bring the day.
Face with good each evil,
Wrath with the soft word,
Smile till stone-faced bigots
Meekly drop their guard.

Chorus: Onward, Christian…

Feeling for each other,
Freely let us move,
Sisters, brothers, partners
In the cause of love;
Celebrating difference,
Recognizing worth;
No one is rejected,
No one trapped by self.

Chorus…

Crowns and thrones must perish,
Power blocks all fall;
One foundation constant,
God's strong love for all;
Ignorance and prejudice
Try to undermine,
God still goes on loving
Past the end of time.

Chorus...

Onward, freedom-seekers,
Set your souls at ease;
You will be composers
Of new harmonies:
Glory without triumph,
Prize with none's defeat;
First the first place taking,
Washing others' feet.

(After Sabine Baring-Gould 1834-1924. Tune: St. Gertrude –
Sullivan. *Faint hearts worried about the word 'comrade' may
sing instead, 'Onward, Christians, onward...')

Out and About For You

Out and about for you we go;
Life in its fullness to explore;
So many friends to make and know,
With every day an open door.

Sometimes a grand assignment given;
Often just routine to fulfil;
Help us in projects small and great,
To sense the honour and the thrill.

Making for oxen easy yokes,
You were a carpenter of fame;
As skilled as ever you design
Our yokes with easy fit, the same.

And if we cannot venture out
Because of sickness, age or care,
We still can work along with you,
And help to bring some change through prayer.

We'll conjure beauty with our smiles
And laughter with our words of cheer;
We'll make some gardens here on earth,
Ready to show the Gardener there!

After Charles Wesley, 'Forth in thy name' tune: Angel's Song -
Orlando Gibbons.

Spread Love and Light

Spread love and light with all your might;
Keep Jesus always in your sight;
Live his full life, and it shall be
Your joy to set the victims free.

Run without weight of spite or hate;
Ready to be the downcast's mate;
Run not to win, or flaunt a prize,
But to bring hope to weary eyes.

Cast care aside; you know your guide;
Jesus will for your needs provide;
Trust him and every day will prove
He holds the keys to life and love.

Don't fret or fear; his arms are near;
His love stands firm, and you are dear.
Let Jesus mean the world to you,
And you will find a purpose true.

(After J.S.B. Monsell 1811-75 'Fight the Good Fight'.)

Tell Us the Good News Story

Tell us the Good News Story,
All other news above,
Of Jesus and his glory -
The glory of his love:
Tell us the story clearly
In accents bold and strong;
Some want us to feel guilty -
They tell the story wrong.

Tell us the Good News Story (x3)
Of Jesus and his love.

Tell us the story slowly
That we may take it in -
Amazing liberation
From dwelling on our sin:
Tell us the story often,
For we so soon lose heart;
Remind us that with Jesus
Each day is a new start.

Tell us... etc.

Tell us the story softly,
With kindness as with zeal;
Remember some have many wounds
That may take long to heal:
Act out the story promptly
If you would seek to be,
To anyone in trouble,

A special friend in need.

Tell us...etc.

Tell us the Good News Story,
When you have cause to fear
That love of self or fortune
Are costing us too dear:
Show us how Jesus' glory
Shines from a loving heart,
And from his love there's nothing
That can hold us apart.

(After Arabella C. Hankey, 1834-1911)

The God of Jesus

The God of Jesus praise,
The God whose name is Love,
The One who speaks to every race,
All worth above.
'I am just what I am',
To Moses God confessed;
See Jesus, God in human frame,
To know the rest.

The God of Jesus praise,
The God with friends galore, -
Boaz and Ruth in ancient days,
And many more.
The 'Shield' of Abraham,
Great David's 'Shepherd-King',
Ezekiel's 'Storm', Isaiah's 'Lamb',
Your praise we sing.

It must be understood,
This God embraces more -
Inspiring Islam's brotherhood
And Buddha's lore.
Great thinkers seek the tracks
Of genius divine, -
The God of Darwin and of Marx,
Freud and Einstein.

God summons us to song,
To vocalize our praise,
Enthuse with fiddle, drum or gong,

And lilting phrase.
Or we may take our part
With brush or sculptor's knife,
And celebrate with work of art
God's feast of life.

The God of Jesus praise,
The God who's yours and mine,
Who guides us through earth's teasing maze
Through cloud and shine.
We shall meet up at last
With Mary, John and Paul;
Jesus will proudly introduce us
- one and all!

(After Thomas Oilvers 1725-99. Sung to Hebrew melody Leoni.)

Morn Was Breaking In

The morn was breaking in,
The holy tent still dark;
The oil lamp burning dim
Before the sacred box,
When suddenly a voice divine
Spoke through the silence of the shrine.

The priest, unkempt, uncouth,
In charge of Shiloh, slept;
Nearby an anxious youth
A wakeful watch still kept;
And what from Eli's sense was sealed,
God unto Hannah's son revealed.*

We envy Samuel's ear,
An open ear, dear God,
Alive and quick to hear
Your whispers, word by word.
Like him we would obey your call,
And stay close to you, most of all.

We envy Samuel's heart,
A patient heart that waits,
Ready your work to start,
Never to help found late;
A heart that always, night or day,
Will not from caring turn away.

But, no, much more we crave,
For Samuel comes not near

One who has love to save
From anger, guilt and fear.
The One who was all hate above
And came to teach us how to love.
(* Hannah was Samuel's mother.)

(After 'Hushed was the evening hymn' J.D.Burns, based on 1 Samuel chapter 3.)

The Sharp Winds of Change

The sharp winds of change are now sweeping our land -
It's you, God, we recognize your Spirit's hand;
She's waking our dull, unadventurous faith,
And nothing is certain or rigid or safe.

(Chorus) Welcome God, welcome new, welcome Spirit again;
In your life, in your love, never one day the same;
We join, as your family, to work and adore,
Your great world to care for, enjoy and explore.

We thank you for leading us right where we are,
For giving the courage to do and to dare,
For lifting our hearts when our feelings were low,
Your laughter to echo, your beauty to show.

Through many a torment and many an ill,
You've led us through valleys and over each hill,
We've marked pleasant vistas and frightening scenes,
But the country we long for will outshine our dreams.

Today you are with us, inspiring our song,
You bind us together to know we belong;
We welcome the sharp winds, disturbing our ways,
Sure sign of your Spirit, God- yours be the praise!

(Inspired by John Gwilym Jones 'Fe chwythodd yr awel..' and
the tune 'To God be the glory' W.H.Doane)

The Son of God Adventures Out

The Son of God adventures out
A hero's fame to win;
His rainbow banner waves aloft,
Who dares to follow him?
Who dares to drink his offered cup
With love filled to the brim?
Who dares to take a rough cross up?
Who dares to follow him?

Steven it was whose angel eye
Could pierce beyond the grave;
He saw his leader in the sky
And called on him to save;
Like Jesus, pardon on his tongue,
As murderers crowded in,
He prayed for those who did the wrong:
Who dares to follow him?

Courageous band, at first a few,
On whom the Spirit came;
Brave or alarmed, their hope they knew
And mocked the cross and flame.
They faced the angry soldier's steel
And in the lion's den
They bowed their necks the death to feel;
Who dares to follow them?

Eternal friends, from every strand
Of rich humanity,
They now before their leader stand

A merry company.
They climbed the steep ascent of heaven
Through peril, pain and sin.
Dear God, may love to us be given
Who dare to follow them.

(After Reginald Heber 1783-1826. 'The Son of God goes forth to war.' Tune: Ellacombe.)

Those Who are Down

Those who are down need fear no fall,
Those who are low no pride;
Those who are humble always will
Have God close by their side.

Let's be content with what we have,
Unless it is too much;
Then we should try to shed the load
Lest conscience lose its touch.

'Carry no pack', our Leader said;
'Whether of goods or care.
My venture will full strength require,
Joy is for those who dare.'

Jesus, life was for you so rough
Yet you found ease of mind.
Teach us the secret in our day
When peace is hard to find.

Help us to mind not what we lose
Or what we fail to gain,
Give thanks for comforts real and not
Make too much of our pain.

Thank you for giving each our cross;
We could not shoulder yours;
As someone helped you bear its weight,
You gladly help with ours.

Those who are down need fear no fall;
You greet them, 'Come in up!'
Those who are humble sit, amazed,
To share your food and cup.

(After John Bunyan 1628-88 Tune: Arden or St. Bernard.)

When We've Christ as a Friend

When we've Christ as our friend
And his words we attend,
What a pleasure we share and display;
While together we plan,
And each does what they can
To help God's New World on its way.

Chorus: *Smile and be free,*
Say, 'I'm glad to be me!'
We're the friends – and not servants-
Jesus wants us to be.

Many shadows will rise;
There'll be clouds in the skies,
And they won't always go the same day;
There'll be doubting and fears
And a fair share of tears,
But our friend holds us tight all the way.

And the closer we walk
And the more that we talk,
The greater the friendship will be;
If no faults are forgiven
There's no love in return,
So don't hide from the one who can see.

There'll be good times as well,
And great stories to tell
With plenty of fine company;
Then we'll see God's World come

And we'll feel quite at home
When those bright merry eyes we first see.

(After J.H. Sammis 1846-1919 'Trust and Obey')

Who Would True Valor See

Who would true valor see -
And bold endeavour -
Mark those whose constancy
Defies all weather;
There's no discouragement
Will make them once relent
Their first avowed intent
To be a pilgrim.

None ever damp their zeal
With dismal stories;
However down they feel,
Their trust the more is;
No bully can them fright,
Nor any giant's might;
They will hold fast their right
To be a pilgrim.

You, loving God, befriend
Us with your Spirit;
We know we at the end
Shall life inherit;
All phantoms fade away;
We fear not what folk say;
We'll each work night and day
To be a pilgrim.

(There is no substitute for Bunyan's poem in the original, which,
in any standard hymnbook, should be set side by side with any

revision. However, since the colourful original - not intended as a hymn - is several cultures away from contemporary perception of reality, revision has to be made if, as a hymn, it is to continue to inspire in a modern setting.)

Worship Your God

Worship your God in the beauty of holiness,
Enter with meekness and wonder proclaim;
Gold of heart's loving and fragrance of lowliness
Bring as your offering, for Love is God's name.

Into God's arms cast your burden of carefulness,
There let it stay as God bears it for you,
Comforts yours sorrows, and answers your prayerfulness,
Guiding your footsteps and seeing you through.

Fear not to come before God in the slenderness
Of the poor wealth you would reckon to own;
Truth in its beauty and joy flecked with tenderness,
These are the presents from loving hearts' home.

Though we may enter in trembling and nervousness,
We'll be received because God holds us dear;
Mornings of joy follow night times of tearfulness,
Trust for our trembling and hope for our fear.

Worship your God in the beauty of holiness,
Enter with reverence and wonder proclaim;
Gold of heart's loving and fragrance of lowliness
Bring as your offering, for Love is God's name.

(after J.S.B. Monsell 1811-75)

You Are The Vision

You are the vision of what I could be,
Companion and Leader,- your love sets me free:
I hold you the first and the last in my heart;
Life will be gloomy if ever we part.

If I need counsel, to you I must go;
When you walk beside me, the best paths you show;
Much closer than brother, more loyal than friend,
Travelling together, right on to the end.

Rid me of weapons and angry displays;
Just help me rely on your methods always:
I need no defence but the truth and the light,
No strength or force but your love shining bright.

Status means nothing, nor wealth or acclaim;
You only my meaning, my value, my fame;
Your care and compassion, your freedom from rules-
These, and these only, I need as my tools.

Jesus, great-hearted, all-glorious in love,
Your gentleness puts you all others above;
I aim to be like you and let you control;
You are my vision: your New World my goal.

(After 'Be thou my vision' – Irish 8th century. Tune: Slane. Set to
these words the last syllable of the 3rd line of each verse is
slurred)

Partnership

Like a Flower

May your love grow like a flower;
Strong to break through frozen ground,
Delicate in tender beauty,
Blooming all the seasons round.
When the wind and storms are raging,
And life's troubles come around,
Help us grow towards your light, Lord,
Where true peace and love are found.

Clothe our lives with your compassion,
May your kindness dress our days,
May love cover over all things,
Bringing harmony and praise,
When we're hurt, help us forgive, Lord,
Showing your forgiving ways;
Help us step into your light, Lord,
Our next step lit by your rays.

Joined together as one body,
May they find the joy love brings;
Each to have and hold the other,
Smiling eyes, and hearts with wings;
Rich or poor, or sick or healthy,
Through the best and worst of things,
Help their lives reflect your light, Lord,
Shining like new wedding rings.

(Simon Walkling) (Tune Calon Lan)

Love Alone

With great pleasure and appreciation I add this 'polished' version of the apostle Paul's great hymn of love to the set. The words are by Stephen Best who wrote them for the occasion of the celebration of his civil partnership and blessing together with his partner Paul at City United Reformed Church 5 May 2006. I was privileged to be present as an invited guest. As with my own efforts there are no copyright rules. Acknowledgement is appreciated.

Any words which I may utter
Without love to reach their goal
Are no more than clashing cymbals
Empty gongs without a soul.
Though I conjure future visions,
Understand life's wherewithal,
And have faith which moves the mountains,
Without love I am not whole.

Acts of charitable giving
And the self-denial call,
If such actions have no loving,
I gain nothing from them all.
Love is patient, love is kindness,
Knows no envy, does not boast,
Bends itself to other's pathways,
Hopes, believes and endures all.

Everything has its own season,
Once a child, I now stand tall.
Though an adult, yet my vision

Through dark mirrors captures all.
While I search for understanding,
Faith and hope and love still call;
And in future generations
Love alone will outlive all.

Stephen Best 2006 (Tune: Blaenwern, or tune to similar metre)

About the Author.

John Henson is a native of Cardiff and a son of the Manse. He graduated in history and theology at the universities of Southampton and Oxford (Regent's Park) respectively and was ordained to the Baptist ministry at Carmel Baptist Church, Pontypridd in 1964. He was responsible for a union between his own church and the United Reformed Church in 1969 (now St. David's, Pontypridd) and has since given assistance to other churches seeking to make similar unions at the local level. He taught history in Cardiff High School from 1970 - 1973 and then resumed ministry at Glyncoch, Pontypridd in cooperation with the Anglican Communion.

Since 1980 he has been largely freelance, acting as pastoral befriender to people in minority groups while continuing to assist in the conduct of worship in the churches. His interests include music, left-wing politics, penal reform, peace, the quest for truly contemporary and inclusive worship and gender issues. A member of the Lesbian and Gay Christian Movement from its early years, for many years he assisted the movement as the contact person for the South Wales group and as a counsellor. He has lectured on faith and gender in Strasbourg and Oslo at the invitation of the European Union and the World Student Christian Federation. He has also lectured in the U.K. at ecumenical conferences and retreat centres, and at Greenbelt. He is also, through 'Facebook', a friend of the Association of Welcoming and Affirming Baptist Churches of the USA. John is happily married to Valerie, his partner for forty-six years. They have three adult children, Gareth, Iestyn and Rhôda, and nine grandchildren- Aidan, Bleddyn, Carys, Gwenllian, Dyfrig, Iona, Isobel, Tomos and Ffion-Medi.

John Henson's books to date are the 'Other' series 'Other Temptations of Jesus', 'Other Communions of Jesus' and 'Other Prayers of Jesus'; "Good-As-New"- translation of the Christian scriptures; 'The Gay Disciple'; and 'Bad Acts of the Apostles'. Still to come will include 'Other Friends of Jesus', 'A Christmas Book', 'The Love Line- scriptural understandings of Gender', and the Welsh language version of ' Good As New'.

BOOKS

O is a symbol of the world, of oneness and unity. In different cultures it also means the "eye," symbolizing knowledge and insight. We aim to publish books that are accessible, constructive and that challenge accepted opinion, both that of academia and the "moral majority."

Our books are available in all good English language bookstores worldwide. If you don't see the book on the shelves ask the bookstore to order it for you, quoting the ISBN number and title. Alternatively you can order online (all major online retail sites carry our titles) or contact the distributor in the relevant country, listed on the copyright page.

See our website **www.o-books.net** for a full list of over 500 titles, growing by 100 a year.

And tune in to myspiritradio.com for our book review radio show, hosted by June-Elleni Laine, where you can listen to the authors discussing their books.

mySpiritRadio